richie manu

YOU:Rebranded
be seen · be heard · get noticed

 **Independent Thinking Press**

First published by
Independent Thinking Press
Crown Buildings, Bancyfelin, Carmarthen, Wales, SA33 5ND, UK
www.independentthinkingpress.com

Independent Thinking Press is an imprint of Crown House Publishing Ltd.

British Library Cataloguing-in-Publication Data.

A catalogue entry for this book is available from the British Library.

Print ISBN 978-1781351383
Mobi ISBN 978-1781352151
ePub ISBN 978-1781352168
ePDF ISBN 978-1781352175

Printed and bound in the UK by
Gomer Press, Llandysul, Ceredigion

For my mum – my first and greatest teacher,

and my worlds, Langlang, Kix and Flish.

Contents

Part 2: **ReAct**

Could establishing your 'skill nucleus' that operates outside of the expectancy and remit of soft and hard skills help to differentiate you but at the same time open up even greater opportunities in business or employment?

It is fundamental to consider the range of devices of communication that perform as satellites, constantly and remotely working for you. It is the strategic management of tangible and intangible factors that are part of your communication, ensuring that you stay in the minds of your network and community, helping you to stay relevant.

Introduction

Me

Allow me to introduce myself. I am Richie Manu – a creative mentor, designer and university lecturer. I have spent all of my working life in the creative industries and have gone through a number of career changes. At each stage, I recognised the importance of reinventing and rebranding myself in order to meet the demands of new challenges. My original passion and interest lay in fine art, but I spent the early years in my career working in graphic design, branding and communications. While I was fairly content in my jobs, I yearned for the creative work that I wasn't always able to do in my day job. While I loved design and branding, what also really drove me was the excitement of merging my interests in music and graphic design.

I had a real interest in acts on the fringe of being signed – I became a 'band chaser'. I remember literally chasing bands and artists that I knew were building followings and getting attention. As a band chaser, I would approach these up-and-coming acts, or their managers, and offer to be their 'design manager': looking after their identity, branding, merchandising and promotions. One of the acts I worked with even gave me a 'free' jacket (as part of my payment) with their name emblazoned on the back. It eventually paid for itself by becoming an automatic backstage pass to their gigs. Result!

Early on in my career, I had to understand and implement fundamental principles that were needed to compete and stand out in a competitive environment and to win and retain business. There were dozens of already established designers and agencies specialising in this area of design for the music industry, so making a mark was bound to be a huge challenge, if not impossible. And yet it was achievable. I continued to freelance as a designer working with start-ups and new enterprises. And as a university lecturer, designer and creative mentor, I now specialise in personal and professional development, working with individuals and organisations to find their voice, to grow and to achieve their targets with effective creative approaches and strategies.

That is the crux of this book: I will share with you some of the tools and strategies that I have learned along the way, including the stories and advice of high-flying professionals from a range of industries who have also related to, adopted and applied these methods with great success.

You

Regardless of where you are in your career, there will be pivotal points when you inevitably face the prospect of challenge and change – from education and employment to entrepreneurship and business. As your roles change, so must you. It is inconceivable that you would stay the same person or maintain the same mindsets and habitual patterns throughout these important stages. In fact, adapting to change, reviewing your thinking and assessing your outlook through these critical times is vital as you progress through your career.

How you create, perceive and react to change is crucial. *You:Rebranded* provides a number of 'lenses' to equip you with the stamina to adapt in today's increasingly fast moving environment, as well as enabling you to challenge traditional conventions of practice and re-navigate your understanding of your value in order to have a positive impact on your career and business opportunities.

Whether you are entering the job market now, have been in employment for years or have aspirations and plans to start your own business, we all have a common objective: to try to stand out from the crowd and communicate our distinctiveness. And that is not easy in an age when everyone is vying for attention and jostling to get to the front of the queue.

There is a lot of noise out there – in both digital and physical environments. And while we might not be able to avoid the noise (and might not want to), the key is figuring out when and how to differentiate ourselves. So, in an age when everyone is shouting, tweeting, screaming, blogging and clamouring for attention, you need to be aware of some of the techniques and approaches that can enhance your characteristics and distinctiveness.

This book is a step towards defining yourself and developing your own authentic voice, enabling you to take a sideways (but forward thinking) look at appraising who you are and where you want to be. You are about to go on a voyage that will take you through the abstract, contrary, thought provoking, alternative, distinctive and informative.

Who are YOU?

You may be among one or more of the following groups:

- The *entrepreneur* or start-up aiming to define and establish yourself.

- The *job hunter* or graduate seeking employment at the start of your career.

- The *career mover* looking for or considering a career change.

- The *ladder climber* seeking promotion in a competitive work environment.

- The *curious* wanting to explore innovative ways to stand out from the crowd.

- The *up and running* – already established but exploring new ways to differentiate yourself from your competitors.

Whoever you are, it is important to recognise the need to change and adapt to new situations and circumstances throughout the various stages of your professional or business career. And as you make your way into new environments, it is vital that you have the tools and knowledge to be able to navigate your way around fresh challenges with confidence. Whatever stage you are at in your career, this book will highlight the essential signposts, experiences and elements that will enhance your progression and distinctiveness.

PART 1
ReThink

1

Digital Watch: Keeping Up with the Times

The information age, along with its social and technological innovations, is impacting on our lives at an exponential rate. Online infrastructure, software applications, computers, hand-held devices, mobile technology, social media and apps have all changed the speed, frequency and way that we interact. When tablets are something we swipe, as well as pop, it becomes clear that technology has also had a significant impact on language, so much so that until recently even a standard spell checker was not happy with the word 'internet'.

Connectivity, interactivity and engagement via digital mediums is now second nature, especially among millennials, and the permeation of technology, communication and social media has changed the way we do everything from purchasing food, dating, job hunting, entertainment, learning, gaming – the list goes on. As 'digital natives',[1] we exist and inhabit the dual environments of the universe and the metaverse, seamlessly floating between physical and virtual existence.

Power shift

The information age, while only a blip in the timeline of the universe, has broken down physical and geographical barriers, including our ability to send messages and communicate globally in a split second. The digital revolution has also shifted the power order from big players to consumers.[2] We have seen it happen in the music industry, with shifts from ownership to streaming access, in gaming and software development and even in the democratisation of publishing, with the popularity of blogs and other online content that can be shared and commented on in seconds.

For the consumer, these changes have broken down barriers rather than supported the big immoveable iron gates of industry. This is the age of the democratisation of knowledge, product and service; it is the world of the bloggers and the empowered, the well-informed

1. This term was coined by Marc Prensky in 'Digital Natives, Digital Immigrants: Part 1', *On the Horizon* 9(5) (2001): 1–6.

2. Roy Greenslade's article on the digital revolution provides an interesting perspective on digital disruption: R. Greenslade, 'How Digital Revolution Gives Power to the People', *London Evening Standard* (6 November 2013). Available at: http://www.standard.co.uk/business/media/roy-greenslade-how-digital-revolution-gives-power-to-the-people-8924261.html.

and well-equipped amateurs.[3] The intersections of various forms of communication also continue to form part of our connective make-up.[4]

There is no doubt that the proliferation of social networks and other digital platforms has had a profound impact on how we communicate, how we are seen, how we are heard and how we get noticed. This also presents an opportunity for us to think, do and say what we do differently, whether employing online tools in the digital space or in offline and physical environments.

Death of the 2D relic?

While digital communication is now prevalent, there are, arguably, still conventional approaches to making an impact. One example is the CV – the curriculum vitae, the résumé, the personal profile; however you wish to label your record of academic, personal and professional achievement. Our history represents a signal to other people who may wish to interact with us, do business with us or hire us about what we might be capable of in the future. But are the days of this 2D relic numbered?

While the CV is a perfectly adequate tool in helping us to progress towards 'the future', much of its content is locked in the past. To a certain extent this is unavoidable: we are using a fixed medium through which to demonstrate past experience and abilities. However (and especially in the wrong hands), the CV can work against us by giving others a perfect excuse to undo our achievements through lack of experience.[5]

While the requirement for a detailed account of academic and professional experience is as vital as ever (there are many professions in which CVs are still an essential part of the recruitment process), the advent of digital technology and connectivity has made it even more critical to transcend A4 paper.[6] Social media platforms, such as

3. In *Creative Disruption*, Simon Waldman observes how digital technologies have had a profound impact on businesses and industry. It features case studies of traditional businesses that have become victims of technological advancement and, in contrast, how technology has also created immense opportunities for businesses, old and new, who have capitalised and gained from the digital revolution: S. Waldman, *Creative Disruption: What You Need to Do to Shake Up Your Business in a Digital World* (Harlow: Financial Times/Prentice Hall, 2010).

4. In their very insightful textbook, *The Communication Age, Connecting and Engaging*, Edwards et al. discuss convergence and the ways in which 'many forms of technologically mediated and face-to-face communication overlap and intersect in our daily lives': A. P. Edwards, C. Edwards, S. T. Wahl and S. A. Myers, *The Communication Age, Connecting and Engaging* (Thousand Oaks, CA: SAGE, 2012), p. 3.

LinkedIn, that enable us to create profiles, connect, interact, discuss and comment are now becoming one of the first stops for prospective employers, clients or business partners.[7]

No magic wand

A simple list of professional experience and evidence of knowledge is no longer enough to compete in today's highly competitive market. New approaches that involve deeper levels of interaction, judgement and critical synthesis are now among the starting points that set individuals and organisations apart. A combination of acquired skills, evidence of application, real-time problem solving and the ability to demonstrate and convey meaning and authenticity in what you have done has increasingly become a standard requirement.

Unfortunately, it is all too common to come across individuals who might as well have rolled up their CV into a tube, waved it around and shouted, 'Abracadabra!', in the hope that a job would magically materialise. The same can also be said for creating an online presence: despite being visually engaging, all too often they can become neglected and out of date. Online and offline profiles are living, breathing entities that demand our constant care and attention. More importantly, they need to convey not only what you have done, but also (and much harder to achieve) to become forward looking – providing information on current projects, problems you have recently solved and conveying critical viewpoints on matters related to your industry.

5. Seth Godin observes: 'If you're remarkable … you probably shouldn't have a résumé at all. A résumé gives the employer everything (s)he needs to reject you. Once you send me the résumé, I can say, "Oh, they're missing this or they're missing that" and boom you're out'. S. Godin, *Linchpin: Are You Indispensable? How to Drive Your Career and Create a Remarkable Future* (London: Piatkus 2010), p. 71.

6. Godin suggests using a blog or projects that an employer can see or touch (ibid.).

7. Lindsey Pollak states that LinkedIn profiles have started to replace CVs and résumés. She believes that in the future employers will rely on professional networking platforms over traditional résumés to make their hiring decisions. L. Pollak, 'The Top Job Search Trends of 2013', *LinkedIn Blog* (14 January 2013). Available at: http://blog. linkedin.com/2013/01/ 14/top-job-search-trends-2013/.

Remember

The growth in digital technology has changed the way we interact. Increasing your channels of communication is essential. Utilise every medium at your disposal to make yourself stand out. However, these mediums are not magic wands and require your constant attention to ensure the information stays relevant and up to date.

Be **Seen**

Understand the power of the digital landscape, its ability to create a wider and more dynamic reach and to generate more opportunities.

Be **Heard**

Use a wide range of mediums to become forward looking and to comment on upcoming projects, your viewpoints and problems you have solved.

Get **Noticed**

The cross-referencing of social, digital and physical platforms presents a great opportunity to think, do and say what you do differently.

2
Quash the Myths

It's not who you know ... it's how many know you

With the growth of social media and social networks, the accumulation of 'friends' in the digital landscape has become a 'likeable' trend in a space where individuals, brands and companies are judged by the rate at which they have generated a mass following. The number of likes, connections and friends has created an environment where likeability is measured by the rate at which people have clicked a button. While social media has expanded the global reach and remit of friends in the digital sphere (although, arguably, the term 'friend' has acquired a new meaning), it has become increasingly apparent that there is still a genuine need to communicate our qualities and attributes to smaller groups – to people who know as much about us as we know about them. Could it be as few as 150 individuals?

In his book, *How Many Friends Does One Person Need?*, the evolutionary anthropologist Robin Dunbar comments on how our world has been redefined by social networking. Some individuals are gathering four-figure numbers of 'friends', many of whom know little or nothing about them.[1] In anthropological studies, he explored the general relationship between size of brain and size of social groupings among primates, including apes, monkeys and humans, of which the natural grouping was 150. This number, known as the Dunbar number, determines the size of our natural groupings and therefore the number of people with whom we can maintain 'meaningful relationships'.[2]

When building and nurturing meaningful relationships and connections in your personal and professional networks, focus not on how many people know you but how much they know about you – thereby ensuring that you communicate your value, skill or expertise to this key smaller grouping. So, if you can only have 150 people in your network, you need to be certain that these individuals are truly connected to you in a reciprocal manner and are aware of your key attributes.

1. Robin Dunbar states: 'the curious by-products of this technological revolution has been a perverse kind of competition about the number of friends you have on your personal site'. R. Dunbar, *How Many Friends Does One Person Need? Dunbar's Number and Other Evolutionary Quirks* (London: Faber and Faber, 2010), p. 21.

2. For more on how Dunbar came up with the concept of the Dunbar number, see: A. Krotoski, 'Robin Dunbar: We Can Only Ever Have 150 Friends At Most ...', *The Observer* (14 March 2010). Available at: http://www.theguardian.com/technology/2010/mar/14/my-bright-idea-robin-dunbar.

Networking without networking

There was a time when networking was solely the domain of the guy who walked into an office with a ton of wires, some leads and a toolbox. Networking was his job, and he was our hero because he knew what kind of leads went into what sockets. Things have changed. Now, when we talk about networking we are usually describing our individual web of personal and professional connections.

Networking is vital for making new associations and developing relationships. If you do it well, you can engineer a complex web of interactions all working for you simultaneously in physical and digital environments. Networking also fosters connectivity: knowledge and ideas are shared within industries, pushing forward innovation and creativity.

While the importance of online professional networking is widely acknowledged, there is a side of networking that is not suited to some individuals (and businesses) who may not be naturally acclimatised to such environments – networking events. Face-to-face interaction remains an essential part of our environment and shapes the way we communicate and interact. However, the space in which some networking happens can be a daunting and sometimes hostile space for the uninitiated. Individuals can be put into bubbles – time capsules which show off their best attributes with the view to drumming up connections, associations and new business in a certain window of opportunity.

A crucial element of networking is networking without necessarily knowing you are networking; the first rule of networking is that you don't talk about networking. For example, explaining what you are working on at the moment or describing something that interests you feels less contrived and more relaxed in the flow of an informal conversation.[3]

3. For more on this, Devora Zack's *Networking for People Who Hate Networking: A Field Guide for Introverts, the Overwhelmed, and the Underconnected* (San Francisco, CA: Berrett-Koehler, 2010) is an interesting read.

You can make networking work for you by:

- Communicating what you do concisely and effectively, leaving a positive and memorable impression that makes people want to interact or do business with you.

- Connecting over common interests to establish links with new people.

- Being confident. It is important to celebrate who you are and not try to be something you are not.

- Being your true authentic self. This makes networking effortless.

- Remembering that you are investing your time and energy – so, make sure it is a good investment that creates positive returns.

There is no box to think outside of

We often encounter the clichéd expression, 'thinking outside the box', in relation to exploring new ideas and creative challenges – essentially thinking differently. It is the uncharted territory we are advised to inhabit to generate innovative solutions. The phrase often lurks in job descriptions, advertising campaigns and creative briefs on the assumption that those who think outside the box are more capable of unconventional thinking and thought processes than those who think within it.

While there are definitely advantages and benefits to thinking differently or divergently, a key attribute is to understand the scope, remit or frame within which you are trying to solve problems or develop new ideas. We are inclined to create our own perceptions of what is meant by being outside the box without interrogating the brief or requirement fully. Furthermore, if everyone is busy thinking outside the box, then outside the box becomes saturated and can frequently lead to predictable outcomes.

This highlights the importance of challenging and questioning terms, conditions and clichés that, by definition, become meaningless without context or elaboration. Not probing or asking informed questions at the right time, and sufficiently early on in the process, can lead to tired solutions that do not reach their full creative potential.

We need to:

- Challenge nebulous terms and content that carry little meaning.

- Conduct research to equip ourselves with knowledge and information, and thereby minimise the chances of failure or rejection.

- Question what is being asked of us in more depth.

- Explore and identify available resources that can help to foster different thinking, such as people or environments.

Despite varying viewpoints on the meaning of the box,[4] the key issue is not whether you are thinking outside it, but more importantly that you position yourself to be able to question the framework within which ideas and processes develop, therefore avoiding predictable paths.

It's probably time we put this box to bed.

Luck is not just reserved for the lucky

Now, before we proceed any further, we are not going to be looking at luck in the context of superstition, rituals, betting odds, probability, lottery or the good fortune of Mr and Mrs Smith from the tiny village of Lucksville who won a packet after entering a multiple choice TV competition, rightly answering that dogs do in fact bark (and not meow or moo, which were the other choices)! Instead, we will focus on the more tangible notion of increasing your opportunities through strategies that get you seen, heard and noticed. So, fingers crossed,

4. Seth Godin states: 'Artists don't think outside the box, because outside the box there's a vacuum. Outside the box, there are no rules, there is no reality. You have nothing to interact with, nothing to work against ... Artists think along the edges of the box, because that's where things get done' (Godin, *Linchpin*, p. 102).

there will be no mention of talismans, charms, horseshoes, shamrocks or any other such luck bringing amulets (touch wood).

To tell or not to tell; surely, that is the equation

Meet Mark. Mark is an aspiring poet. He is young, passionate about his craft and spends much of his free time writing poetry. He has amassed hundreds of poems, all of which are based on a combination of personal experience, observation and travels. Friends and colleagues think that he should publish his poems in a book or consider giving voice to his words by performing to small audiences. However, Mark already has a full-time job and finds it very difficult to devote enough time to getting out there and promoting himself. After years of side-lining his passion, he now fears his poetry may be just an elaborate pastime dressed up as a hobby rather than a possible future career.

Mark is an example of a prolific creative who, because of limited networks, lack of exposure and connections, lacks confidence and stops at the first hurdle without taking his ambitions any further. There is a good argument that the more people who know about what you do, the more chance you have of success or progression, further increasing your opportunities and word of mouth recommendation. But it requires action: moving beyond your mastery or craft and making connections with networks and experiences.

If you can relate to Mark's situation, you should consider:

- Increasing your exposure: make the most of your social media profiles and networks.

- Building your confidence: get feedback from trusted friends and family, or try debuting your project to a wider audience.

- Developing connections with established people in your field.

There are many theories about luck and chance. Jason Roberts is an entrepreneur from California who coined the phrase 'Luck Surface Area'. This is 'directly proportional to the degree to which you do something you're passionate about combined with the total number of people to whom this is effectively communicated. It's a simple concept, but an extremely powerful one because what it implies is that you can directly control the amount of luck you receive. In other words, you make your own luck.'[5]

Roberts formalises this into an equation, $L = D*T$ (L represents luck, D represents Doing and T represents Telling), and a corresponding graph (see below). Simply put, the more you do, and the more you connect with networks and individuals, the more your Luck Surface Area is increased. So, in Mark's case, he has plenty of D but clearly not enough T, thus his Luck Surface Area is compromised.

The Telling includes self-promotion, informing, networking, performing, connecting, marketing, social media and so on. No simple thing, for sure, but you can start to see where Mark could increase his Luck Surface Area. Although this is not a scientifically proven application, the diagram provides an indication of the contrast between ideation and implementation to create impact and engagement.

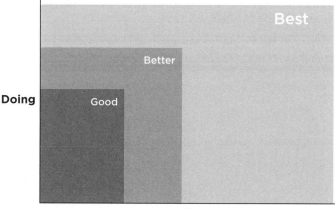

Doing

Best

Better

Good

Telling

5. J. Roberts, 'How to Increase Your Luck Surface Area', *Codus Operandi* (2010). Available at: http://www.codusoperandi.com/posts/increasing-your-luck-surface-area.

Consider the scope of your current Doing and Telling and plot on the graph where you think you are at the moment. Is this where you want to be? If not, make a mark where you would like to be. What steps will be required to get from where you are to this point?

Charlotte goes from 30° to zero°

Charlotte, a young journalist and regional news presenter, was invited to a panel discussion to debate the issue of youth unemployment. At a small drinks reception after the event, she spoke with a member of the audience and they explored further the difficulties that young people face when entering the job market.

The young man asked Charlotte about her own career path, commenting on her level of success at a local television network. 'It's very competitive to become a news presenter on television. You were really lucky to have landed that job,' said the young man. You could have heard a pin drop. The atmosphere turned chilly. 'It certainly wasn't luck!' replied Charlotte. 'It was years of hard work, fighting against the odds, pushing for promotions, late nights, sacrifice of quality time, commitment and sheer downright grit. Does that sound like luck to you?' Clearly, Charlotte felt that the notion of 'luck' negated and devalued all her hard work and years of dedication.

However, according to a leading psychologist, there are scientifically proven ways to increase your luck and thereby increase your opportunities. Professor Richard Wiseman asserts that people are not born lucky but can generate their own good fortune by using four main principles:

1. Maximise your chance opportunities.

2. Listen to your luck hunches.

3. Expect good fortune.

4. Turn your bad luck into good.[6]

6. See Richard Wiseman, *The Luck Factor: The Scientific Study of the Luck Mind* (London: Arrow, 2004).

In an article for the *Skeptical Inquirer*, he says: 'They [lucky people] are skilled at creating and noticing chance opportunities, make lucky decisions by listening to their intuition, create self-fulfilling prophesies via positive expectations, and adopt a resilient attitude that transforms bad luck into good.'[7]

Remember

Whether you are an advocate of the Luck Surface Area or adhere to Wiseman's four principles, you cannot rely solely on skill and talent alone. Good luck – let's move on.

Be **Seen**

Make people aware of you and what you do through your online and face-to-face networks.

Be **Heard**

There are a lot of people trying to raise their voice above the crowd. Make sure your message is clear, positive and memorable.

Get **Noticed**

Whether you call it luck or not, making the most of opportunities to meet people and share your ideas will help to get you noticed.

7. R. Wiseman, 'The Luck Factor', *Skeptical Inquirer* (May/June 2003). Available at: http://richardwiseman.files.wordpress.com/2011/09/the_luck_factor.pdf. See also Daniel Pink, 'How to Make Your Own Luck' [interview with Richard Wiseman], *Fast Company* (30 June 2010). Available at: www.fastcompany.com/46732/how-make-your-own-luck.

3
The Dream-Breaker

The unexpected twist in the tale of the brilliant employee

John works in fashion retail. John is a brilliant employee. His colleagues look up to him not only because he is good but because he is one of the longest serving members of staff. He is the old kid on the block. He is non-confrontational, diplomatic and agreeable, which makes for an easier life for John and all those around him. He is often the last to leave the office and one of the first to sign up for staff training courses because he wants to stay ahead and keep his knowledge current. He loves his job and feels comfortable, settled and part of the establishment. He is often referred to as 'The Walking Job Description'. He is happy, content and genuinely feels that he has a job for life. Secure, warm, cosy.

But it wasn't always that way. Zoom back a few years and John had fire in his belly. With a degree in fashion design, he dreamed of starting up his own small fashion label focusing on t-shirts featuring the artwork of local artists. He considered going into partnership with someone else, as he didn't feel he had a business brain (or a business plan), but he had a clear vision and passion. He had done his research and started to make connections with established people in the industry.

As much as he dreamed of making this enterprise work, his day job was keeping him fully occupied. In a full-time 9 to 5 role, most of his time during the week was monopolised by his job, and he found it difficult to make any significant progress on developing his own idea. However, he was relatively happy to keep his ideas on ice knowing that one day he would find the time to develop his plan.

Zoom forward, back to real time ...

Unprepared for an 'alien' invasion

There are rumours of changes in the company that will affect jobs and the business structure. John doesn't seem worried. He is due for a sabbatical following his long years of service, so he hopes all this talk of change and possible lay-offs will have died down by the time he returns. After all, his job is secure, warm, cosy.

John takes his sabbatical and is away for three months, which is a lifetime in any organisation. On his first day back, he can't help but notice how much the workplace has changed. Not only in its design, layout and structure, but also the personnel and internal behaviours. In John's mind, the 'aliens' have landed. They speak in code, acronyms and abbreviations. They smell of new systems, processes and innovation.

Things are not as they were. As much as John tries to adapt to this new environment, he is aware of the pressures of staying relevant (and staying employed). He never thought he would hear himself say it, but he thinks it's time to leave the company and consider looking for another role in fashion retail. He starts his hunt for a new job – to find another secure, warm, cosy company. But he discovers how difficult it is to find similar positions that match his experience and skills. While his years of service are relatively creditable in his current company, he can't convert that expertise into interviews or opportunities.

And the dream? The dream remained sadly dormant. It screamed for his attention, devotion and commitment. But it couldn't compete against his inner voice that told him his job was secure, that he was doing well and that the time wasn't right. Although his dream of starting up his own small label was never far away, he gradually lost his passion and zest.

John was under the illusion that he was working in a relatively safe and secure environment, but his perception couldn't have been further from the truth. John never looked out of the window. He was so preoccupied that he failed to see that he had built his own ivory tower. He was working in a bubble that actually disconnected him from the industry beyond his job, as well as his own ambitions. By the time he was ready to do something about it, he had created a comfort zone around himself such that what appeared to be career progression was in fact contributing to him keeping his eye off his own business vision.

Investing in the vision

Regardless of what stage you are at in your career, it is important to focus on your long-term ambitions. There are many obstacles and dream-breakers that will challenge your commitment and desire, so your resilience to the forces that threaten to dilute your vision and aspiration to a mere hobby must be strengthened. This requires a mindset that resists dividing your time between work and interests and refocuses on a plurality of the mind.

The demands and stresses of maintaining a healthy work–life balance can be very challenging. However, there are ways to ensure that the plurality starts to work residually for you – for instance, creating a multifaceted ring of touch-points that form part of your identity both physically (e.g. talks, events, networking) and virtually (e.g. website, blogs, online profile).

Investing in your future (and not only financially) is fundamental. The time you commit to, for example, developing your online profile, holding an event, starting a blog or developing a product (even at beta stage) are all steps in a positive direction to realising your goal.[1]

By the way, John did eventually find a new role in another organisation and also continued to invest in his dream to develop his own t-shirt brand in collaboration with artists.

1. Randy Pennington highlights the importance of strategically investing in your future: 'People who purchase your product or service are asking, "Why you? Why now? What makes you relevant?" Employers who are deciding to hire you or even keep you on the payroll are asking the same questions … The best in every field of endeavor actively manage their futures.' R. Pennington, *Make Change Work: Staying Nimble, Relevant, and Engaged in a World of Constant Change* (Hoboken, NJ: John Wiley & Sons, 2013), p. 10.

Remember

It can be hard to reconcile your aspirations and your immediate prospects. The warm, cosy job can be great, but don't confuse secure with safe and stultifying.

Be **Seen**

Don't lose sight of your ambitions. Make the most of the opportunities your current role or company offers you, but don't neglect the bigger picture.

Be **Heard**

The importance of listening to yourself cannot be understated. Trust your instincts and don't let unhelpful voices shout louder than your dreams. Settling for something 'for now' is not the same as giving up.

Get **Noticed**

If you aren't doing anything to pursue your ambitions, how is anyone else going to take notice?

4
Curiosity Didn't Kill the Cat

The curious being

In order to discover how curiosity can impact on your career or professional development, it is essential to acknowledge it as a state of being, not doing. You cannot *perform* the act of being curious; it requires you to *be* curious. The acknowledgment of curiosity as a state of being, rather than something you do, means that your receptors are constantly on call.

Curious people share common traits that help to define them but which also highlight their interest and wonder. These include the characteristics of intensity, frequency and durability.[1] While these point us towards some fundamental human attributes, they also highlight the fact that a curious nature needs constant stimulation in order to cultivate and nourish new ideas.

The diagram below indicates the disparity between curiosity and being curious.

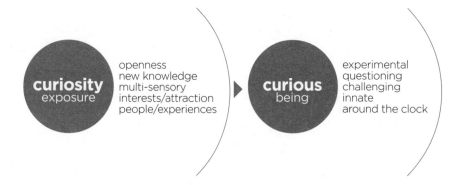

curiosity
exposure

openness
new knowledge
multi-sensory
interests/attraction
people/experiences

curious
being

experimental
questioning
challenging
innate
around the clock

1. Todd Kashdan identifies the qualities that make up the curious person: 'The first quality is intensity. Highly curious people feel more intense feelings of curiosity, interest and wonder ... The more curious among us are open to new experiences, even when familiar and secure ideas and routes are challenged. The second quality is frequency. Highly curious people feel curious many times in a given day ... The third quality is durability. A curious person's sense of intrigue and desire to explore often endures for lengthier periods of times.' T. Kashdan, *Curious? Discover the Missing Ingredient to a Fulfilling Life* (New York: HarperCollins, 2009), p. 31.

Bigger questions

Albert Einstein's determination to investigate, search, question and explore was as important to him as finding the answers. He is famously quoted as saying, 'I have no special talent. I am only passionately curious'. The whole idea of curiosity can involve mind-expanding encounters and experiences that bring with them new adventures and new knowledge – and all this before we have even arrived at any answers. Curiosity is innately embedded in questions rather than answers. When we truly begin to understand this, we become less solution focused, thereby inducing better questions that bring us closer to better answers. The true worth of questions cannot be underestimated. Creativity and innovation are arguably driven by an investigative attitude where better or more challenging questions aid and do not hinder the creative process.[2]

At a basic level, curiosity is an emotion, a state of being, a behaviour that manifests from a strong desire to learn or to find something new and informative.[3] In order to become more curious we need to want to know more – and with curiosity comes new knowledge. It is a self-fulfilling process.

Within the context of differentiation, curiosity has the ability to set us apart. It is one of the most important factors in the nurturing of new discoveries that ultimately contribute to defining us. Our curiosity for culture, food, social and psychological behaviour, relationships, love, travel, art, architecture, among many other things, will yield a very distinctive combination of experiences that shape the way we act, live and think as individuals. But in order to yield positive rewards and outcomes we need to be open to new experiences.

2. In an interview, Tim Brown, chief executive of IDEO, observes: 'it doesn't matter how good the answers you come up with. If you're focusing on the wrong questions, you're not really providing the leadership you should ... probably the most important role we can play is asking the right questions.' A. Byrant, 'He Prizes Questions More Than Answers' [interview with Tim Brown], *New York Times* (24 October 2009). Available at: http://www.nytimes.com/2009/10/25/business/25corner.html?pagewanted=all.

3. Todd Kashdan states: 'We are open and receptive to finding opportunities, making discoveries, and adding to the meaning in our life ... By being open and curious in our moments we can improve even the most mundane aspects of our daily routine' (Kashdan, *Curious?*, p. 4).

The ocean that leads to 'openness'

For decades, psychologists have agreed that there are five key personality traits or dimensions. Often referred to as the 'Big Five' or the Factor Five Model, these are openness, conscientiousness, extraversion, agreeableness and neuroticism (of which OCEAN is the most commonly used acronym). These descriptions derive from analyses of the terms people use to describe themselves and others.[4]

Among these traits, openness draws significant links with curiosity and being receptive to new and unfamiliar experiences. When we become more curious, we also open up the bandwidth of the events, activities and challenges that we experience. These go on to create distinctive combinations of experiences that make us stand out.[5]

While it is clear that an open-minded outlook can yield greater opportunities and experiences, it is also important that this is driven by a genuine desire to make new discoveries that are aligned with our meaning and purpose. In terms of professional development, it always helps to keep your longer term objectives and goals in mind. While the spirit of curiosity might advocate a broad reach and freedom to the experiences you seek, there is value in ensuring that those experiences are relevant to your career or personal objectives.

That said, it is beneficial to seek out learning experiences in related or selected industries, acquiring novel insights about developments and trends that you can bring back to inform your own objectives. While these factors might have a significant effect on your accumulated knowledge of an alternative industry, they might also have a profound impact on shaping and differentiating you.

4. See O. P. John and S. Srivastava, 'The Big-Five Trait Taxonomy: History, Measurement and Theoretical Perspectives' (University of California at Berkeley, 1999). Available at: http://pages.uoregon.edu/sanjay/pubs/bigfive.pdf.

5. Todd Kashdan suggests that 'Openness can be considered a hodge podge of ingredients ... people who are open extract greater pleasure from variety and novelty' (Kashdan, *Curious?*, p. 291).

Through a child's eye

Much of the discussion on curiosity suggests that, in order to activate our curiosity, we need to connect with our 'inner child'.[6] Children are naturally curious: they question to discover and learn. They have a tendency to ask some of the toughest questions: why is the sky blue? What is the condensation on the inside of a window? What exactly is a megapixel? Why do we itch? (I have been asked all of these questions and have had no immediate answer other than 'Because it is' or 'I'll get back to you on that one'!) It's amazing that children will find thousands of uses for a cardboard box. They create play with the simplest of objects and invent stories from whatever is around them – such as a dog chasing a rabbit inspired by cloud formations.

Through play and learning, children engage multiple senses simultaneously as they explore new territories. They prod, push, bend, throw, smell, taste, listen, feel. If you have observed children at play, consider how much of their time is spent trying to find answers. Almost none. They are on a constant quest driven mainly by an inquisitive mind that isn't afraid of being wrong or judged. As we get older, our desire to conform and fit in diminishes our curiosity. We explore less, we ask fewer questions and we work to set rules, tasks and objectives that leave little or no room to question convention.[7]

Transformation through curiosity

In a study conducted by Harvard psychologist Ellen Langer, a group of volunteers were asked to prepare speeches for an audience. The objective was to understand how curiosity can transform anxiety. The volunteers were divided into three groups. One group was asked to make no mistakes; the second group was told mistakes would be excused; and the third group was told that they could liberally make

6. See, for example, S. Magsamen, 'How to Embrace Your Inner Child', *Oprah* (27 October 2009). Available at: http://www.oprah.com/spirit/How-to-Embrace-Your-Inner-Child-Sandra-Magsamen.

7. In a TED talk, Sir Ken Robinson observes, 'kids will take a chance. If they don't know, they'll have a go. They're not frightened of being wrong ... And by the time they get to be adults, most kids have lost that capacity. They have become frightened of being wrong ... We stigmatise mistakes.' K. Robinson, 'How Schools Kill Creativity' [video], TED (February 2006). Available at: http://www.ted.com/talks/ken_robinson_says_schools_kill_creativity?language=en.

mistakes, even incorporating mistakes into their speech. Surprisingly, the third group (according to the audience) delivered the most composed, effective and articulate speeches of the three. This group were also most comfortable with the exercise.[8]

So, a restricted and anxious mind becomes less creative, less productive and more inhibited. We might also observe that cultivating a positive attitude to failure can be driven by a curiosity to discover how to make the best out of situations – and that includes learning from mistakes to inform our development.

Expanding your curiosity bandwidth

Expanding your curiosity bandwidth can reap many rewards (see the diagram below). Think about some of the aspects of your environment that you might take for granted, no matter how simple or trivial, and

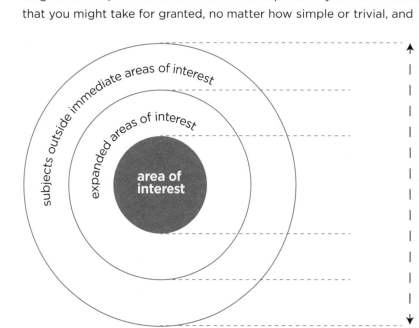

curiosity bandwidth

8. For more on this see: R. Ifould, 'Curiosity: The Secret to Your Success', *Psychologies* (16 January 2013). Available at: https://psychologies. co.uk/self/curiosity-the- secret-to-your-success. html or visit http://www. ellenlanger.com/.

with a child's eye ask yourself some tough or challenging questions. You could also look at immediate areas of interest from a new perspective – for example, if you have an interest in art, explore new disciplines or media. Looking outside the perimeter of your immediate interests will expand your horizons and may also widen your networks.

Curiosity around the clock

Simply becoming more curious as a reactive or temporary measure is counterproductive and counterintuitive. Curiosity is a mindset that needs regular practice to become part of your natural behaviour. Curiosity doesn't have an off-switch either. It requires constant connectivity – such as appreciating the value in things you might take for granted in your everyday life, such as colour, shape and form.

More than just maintaining an open mind, curiosity can also challenge us to engage with numerous senses simultaneously to open up new experiences and insights. It encourages experiments in taste, sound, tactility, smells and visual stimulation. It can be interesting to explore how the cross-pollination and interplay of the senses can generate new understanding. For example, food can engage us on a number of levels, stimulating the senses of touch, sight, taste and smell. Consider what other experiences you can engage with that, in turn, may develop new insights.

Curiosity beyond the comfort zone

While curiosity might draw you to things that interest you, it is hugely beneficial to explore areas outside of your existing interests to expand your mind and develop new insights that can then inform your practice. Chapter 17 will consider the importance of expanding your skill set by investigating areas outside of your sphere of expertise. It also looks briefly at skill projection and how you can re-channel your skills for new industries. Applying this 'future lens' requires inquisitiveness in sectors way beyond the remit of your field of expertise. However, this process of engaging with the unfamiliar can open up new and exciting opportunities.

Remember

Curiosity should be seen as a behaviour but, more importantly, as a state of being in which your receptors are constantly at work, engaging a multitude of senses.

Be **Seen**

The more you can demonstrate an active curiosity, the more you will attract and inspire people with a shared vision.

Be **Heard**

Be vocal about the things that interest you and reflect on those new experiences. In this way you will avoid them going into a vault.

Get **Noticed**

Expanding your curiosity bandwidth can unveil new landscapes in which you open up novel associations and networks. By being curious you are also creating room for discussions that will enable you to communicate your interests and objectives.

5

The Virtue of Failure

Reframing failure

Look up 'fail' or 'failure' in the dictionary and you will find, of course, that the definition is packed with many terms associated with not being successful and not achieving your objectives. As an antonym of either 'pass' or 'success', it is understandable why there is no room for failure in the vocabulary of individuals who want to succeed and achieve their ambitions.

Try telling an athlete, a footballer or even a learner driver on their sixth driving test that failure is part of the learning process and you will probably get a negative reaction. However, the ability to analyse, reflect and learn from failure without it halting or hindering progress is a vital skill. It requires us to reframe and reposition certain aspects of failure so that any positive factors can be extrapolated and used constructively.

Misadventure is often perceived as being a contributory factor to the ultimate success of many business entrepreneurs and other high-achieving figures – from the multimillionaire who lost thousands, dusted herself off and remade a fortune, to the rags-to-riches individual who turned around a failed education to become the richest kid on the block. A common thread is their ability to take a different slant on failure and to keep going, seeing opportunities where others would have seen last base.[1]

The idea of failure can carry with it many negative associations that make it difficult to also see it as a valuable learning experience. It is often seen as a final destination, rather than recognised as an important learning tool or stepping stone that brings you closer to a solution. It is your attitude to failure, and your ability to draw on new perspectives, that will transform it from a negative to a positive.[2] Embrace it as part of your journey.

1. Vera Peiffer points to techniques that enable individuals to rethink classic negative thoughts and convert them into positive outcomes. She also highlights an important link with the self-fulfilling prophecy: 'you will act out that belief; because you do not tackle any new situations you feel like a failure, and therefore you fail'. V. Peiffer, *Positive Thinking: Everything You Have Always Known About Positive Thinking But Were Afraid to Put into Practice* (London: HarperCollins, 2002), p. 7.

2. In an interview, Silicon Valley serial entrepreneur Steve Blank discussed how in an early venture, despite losing US$35 million in investor funding, he eventually went on to earn US$1 billion for each investor. He said: 'Learning from that failure for me was one of the best experiences of my life ... "experience" is simply another word for "failure".' J. Porter, 'How Failure Made These Entrepreneurs Millions', *Entrepreneur* (14 June 2013). Available at: http://www.entrepreneur.com/article/227011.

A brief enlightening history on failure

The year is 1876. In New Jersey, a young unknown 29-year-old inventor has set up an ideas lab. Under his stewardship, he and his team have developed hundreds of ideas, one of which is the world's first commercially viable light bulb. He famously (allegedly) says, 'I have not failed 1,000 times. I have successfully discovered 1,000 ways to not make a light bulb.' His name is Thomas Edison.[3]

For countless decades, many had tried (and failed) to develop a light source that lasted for more than a few minutes. It was Edison, however, who created a marketable product that burned for much longer than its predecessors. It is important to note that the developmental achievements of Edison's predecessors were also pivotal in the evolution of the light bulb. So, recognising failure as a learning experience and contributory factor towards eventual success means taking a totally different perspective on process and the iterative stages of development.[4]

Dissecting the beast

When failure occurs, dealing with discouragement or criticism can be an obstacle. Being able to reflect and act positively on negative feedback is an important attribute. It is imperative to dissect the feedback, break it down into manageable chunks, analyse these carefully and develop a plan of action for the future. Reflection will give you signposts for further development – it is the glue that will connect subsequent stages.

The following points are crucial when reflecting on and analysing failure:

• Allow space and time for reflection and contemplation.

• Develop an overview of the perceived failure and gain some sense of its scope or magnitude.

3. Contrary to popular belief, Edison was not the inventor of the light bulb. As early as 1809, Sir Humphry Davy, an English physician, had made a breakthrough by making an electrical connection between two charcoal rods connected to a power source and eventually created what was known as the Arc Lamp. Innovator Joseph Swan received a British patent for his light bulb in around 1878 and by the early 1880s he had started his own light bulb company. For more on this see: http://www.lightbulb.co.uk/who-invented-the-light-bulb.html.

4. British inventor James Dyson famously made over 5,000 prototypes before getting his 'bagless' vacuum cleaner right: 'I made 5,127 prototypes of my vacuum before I got it right. There were 5,126 failures. But I learned from each one … So I don't mind failure.' See C. Salter, 'Failure Doesn't Suck' [interview with James Dyson], *Fast Company* (1 May 2007). Available at: http://www.fastcompany.com/59549/failure-doesnt-suck.

- As well as asking, 'Where did it go wrong?' it is important to focus on what went right, as these elements will feed into the next stages.

- Avoid 'error blindness' by recognising and accepting what went wrong.[5]

- Understand the distinction between 'good failure' and 'bad failure' to ensure that setbacks are seen as 'iterative and constructive' instead of 'regressive and destructive'.[6]

- Consider what new resources or restructuring are required as part of the review.

The diagram below represents the polarity between iterative failures that lead to increased knowledge or learning and unproductive failures that lead to no increased knowledge or learning.

Failure polarity

'iterative and constructive'

- ongoing work in progress
- accumulative stages
- each step informing the next
- recorded, reflected, analysed, reviewed

'regressive and destructive'

- mismanagement of resources
- failure to plan and measure
- underestimating time and commitment
- inconsistency

5. In a TED talk on aspects of 'being wrong', Kathryn Schulz comments on getting stuck inside a feeling of rightness: 'I call this error blindness. Most of the time, we don't have any kind of internal cue to let us know that we're wrong about something, until it's too late.' K. Schulz, 'On Being Wrong' [video], *TED* (March 2011). Available at: http://www.ted.com/talks/kathryn_schulz_on_being_wrong?language=en.

6. Don Reinertsen discusses how our reaction to failure depends very much on what we mean by failure in his article, 'Try to Understand the Difference between Good and Bad Failures', *Electronic Design* (1 May 2000). Available at: http://electronicdesign.com/archive/try-understand-difference-between-good-and-bad-failures.

Lab thinking

The laboratory is principally an environment where experimentation, testing, research, exploration and creativity take place, and it is typically the domain of scientists, physicians and other medical professionals. Outside the remit of science and medicine, we can all adopt a mindset of 'lab thinking' when it is important to develop an open attitude to trial and error as part of the trajectory of success.

At the heart of lab thinking there is an attitude of:

- Building a 'What if?' approach to experimentation that is compounded by a genuine desire to explore the unknown.

- Accepting risk taking as part of the experimental landscape.

- Not being solution focused but allowing room for error, mistake, iteration and testing.

- Facilitating and accommodating change.

Lab thinking encourages us to work within an experimental framework of enquiry, where questioning does not hinder but, in fact, facilitates the process. When we stop expecting to find the perfect answer immediately, we open up the curiosity bandwidth to more ideas that can be tested, rejected and developed.

Remember

It is imperative to reframe your understanding of failure as progressive. However, it is also fundamental to make clear distinctions between 'iterative and constructive' failure and 'regressive and destructive' failure. Reflection is also important as part of the analysis of failure.

Be **Seen**

Depending on the nature of your expertise, being open about some of the shortcomings in your progress could invite collaborations and new partnerships.

Be **Heard**

People are receptive to learning about process and how you got there, as well as the solution or end product. Ensure, wherever possible, that you are transparent about process and communicate this effectively so that it is recognised as a positive aspect of the journey.

Get **Noticed**

Experimentation and risk taking may become part of your profile. This should not be confused with the haphazard, but there is certainly a virtue in being renowned when experimentation and failure have played a major part of the outcome. (The out-takes at the end of the *Airplane* movies are arguably as memorable as the films themselves!)

6

Ditch Noddy – Date the Devil's Advocate

It is natural to seek praise and encouragement, but it is equally important to elicit a critical perspective. While agreement and acceptance are always a good thing, you need to test your ideas on groups or audiences that have no inhibitions about providing honest, transparent feedback. It is important to harness the value of constructive critical feedback and comments. Embracing and working with concrete reactions can offer a clear path for future development.

Developing a reliable and informative sounding board for ideas is vital in the progression of early concepts. But, whether you are at the start of a project, mid development or near completion, it is crucial that your audience, as well as the questions you ask, challenge you to achieve your objectives. While it is tempting to turn to familiar groups or individuals that we know will provide a safe haven for our embryonic ideas, it is even more important to elicit feedback from folks outside of our immediate circle of familiarity.

Tougher audience, tougher questions, better answers

Road-testing our ideas effectively comes down to not only the questions we ask but also who we ask. The way in which we frame and contextualise our questions, whether consciously or unconsciously, can provoke primarily positive responses. While cheering to our ego, if reactions do not challenge they create limited room for growth and development. This is usually the result of asking questions which we already have the (predictable) answer to or drawing out the answers we might want to hear.

It is advantageous if close friends, family, colleagues and companions within your network who have experienced the various stages of your ambitions can be supportive and constructive, without holding back for fear of upsetting you. Set clear parameters and simply ask recipients to be as candid as possible in their responses.

It is beneficial to go through a mental checklist when evaluating your questions and/or responses:

- Have you asked the right questions? Are they challenging enough?

- Have you challenged yourself enough if the feedback is looking too positive?

- Have you set appropriate parameters within which to obtain feedback?

Hello stranger ...

So, how do we strike an effective balance between eliciting positive (and not necessarily constructive) feedback from those closest to us and subjecting our ideas to people who might potentially have a discouraging effect on the development of an idea? One approach is to think from the outside in, by testing ideas and concepts on those in our more immediate circles only after they have been exposed and subjected to evaluation from an outer circle of strangers and devil's advocates.

This may seem like a daunting prospect, especially if you don't feel ready to take your incomplete ideas or work in progress to an unfamiliar audience. However, subjecting the early stages of your plans or thought processes to a critical audience can open you up to a totally new dimension of thinking. These 'strangers' need not, of course, be total strangers but could be leading experts, established figures in your field or trusted sources in affiliated organisations. Approaching industry professionals both within and beyond your area of expertise, or even from a very broad demographic (depending on what you are seeking an opinion on) can be very beneficial. It can also provide mind-expanding insights that may shape the development of your thinking or concept.[1]

1. In *Making Ideas Happen*, Scott Belsky describes taking ideas from outside your community – what he calls 'idea intoxication'. This involves engaging with cynical and risk-averse individuals who generate useful chemistry in the creative and thinking process: 'You need to work with people who ask the difficult, practical questions that are frustrating but important when pushing ideas forward.' S. Belsky, *Making Ideas Happen: Overcoming the Obstacles Between Vision and Reality* (New York: Penguin, 2009), p. 159.

Not just critical but holistic

Engaging with the devil's advocate is not just about gaining a more critical perspective, but obtaining a more holistic viewpoint on your ideas:

- Focus – it is important to retain a focused vision that is concerned with how ideas can be improved (and less so on the likeability or aesthetic appeal of a project).

- Broaden the range of your devil's advocates – consider how different audiences could give you constructive criticism.

- Be clear on what you want feedback on – depending on the nature of your enquiry, you may need to ascertain or identify parameters to ensure you get purposeful and insightful feedback (e.g. aesthetics, functionality, infrastructure).

- Your recipients need to be aware of their role as devil's advocates to ensure that they understand that their criticality will be received as valuable rather than discouraging.

Little black hat

Edward de Bono is often hailed as the father of lateral thinking and creativity. As well as his numerous publications, he has devised methods and tools to foster and encourage creative thinking. One of his more well-known strategies is Six Thinking Hats, which is a simple but effective process to enable individuals and groups to think more coherently and to be more productive.[2] Different coloured hats are used to represent different thinking approaches. Each hat (white, yellow, black, red, green, blue) gives individuals and groups free licence to think within the parameters of their given hat.

The black hat encourages critical thinking in order to detect shortcomings, negative aspects, limitations, gaps and threats in a project:

2. Visit http://www.edwdebono.com/ for a detailed account of the Six Thinking Hats process and more on de Bono's work.

> *The Black Hat is judgment – the devil's advocate or why something may not work. Spot the difficulties and dangers; where things might go wrong. Probably the most powerful and useful of the Hats but a problem if overused.*[3]

While the devil's advocate strategy is useful in the context of brainstorming or problem solving, for teams as well as individuals, there is also value in using it to seek new and critical perspectives on career and/or professional development.

Light at the end of the tunnel

Whether you adopt a degree of critical thinking yourself or appoint a group of devil's advocates, it is important to adopt an unconventional perspective on the questions you are asking yourself, or others, in order to meet your objectives. For example, try to go beyond just prompting an opinion and drill down into how an idea can be improved or where the gaps and flaws are. Aim to remain motivated and positive during this process, as it is not uncommon for negative viewpoints to slow down or even halt progress altogether.

Here are some key principles to bear in mind when addressing any discouraging issues brought up during this process:

- Embrace feedback – while your objectives will be fuelled by dedication and passion, it is important that you also have a steely reserve that can embrace constructive criticism.

- Be open-minded – criticality requires a thick skin but also a high degree of open-mindedness, adaptability and agreeableness.

- Avoid U-turns – this is, without doubt, the part of the journey where negative feedback is most likely to check progress.

3. See http://www.
debonogroup.com/six_
thinking_hats.php.

- See the light – even negative feedback should be seen as a step in the right direction. The key is to understand the criticism and resolve how to act on it.

To like or not to like – there is the button

Talks, conferences, debates, panel discussions, articles, meet-ups and many other platforms that once only occupied a physical space now get our attention in digital environments where we have a potential audience of millions. The internet and mobile technologies continue to have a huge impact on how, when and where we communicate and share ideas. Blogs, YouTube, Pinterest, Facebook, podcasts, webinars, Twitter and Instagram are all valuable channels for communicating our thoughts, opinions, ideas and concepts.

From the 'like' button to the comment box, it is essential that meaning is extrapolated and processed so that feedback and comments can truly shape and develop our character and distinctiveness. The internet has enabled the sharing and evaluating of ideas and opinions with relatively 'unknown' groups via tools such as Google+. This enables us to direct focused questions to particular audiences or focus groups and thereby obtain distilled feedback.

We can even engage with multiple mediums synchronically to obtain comments and feedback, to discuss and debate. However, it is fundamental that we process, filter, analyse and make valid judgements on any criticism we receive, whether it has emerged from a physical or digital environment. Surveys, questionnaires and polls are pointless if they do not yield results that can better inform our process.

Remember

Gaining new insights starts with you being your harshest critic. The better and tougher your questions, the better the responses. Industry professionals or leading experts can play a huge role in providing honest feedback.

Be **Seen**

You should be prepared to unveil your concepts and ideas inside and outside your community. But insist on useful and critical feedback that is designed to genuinely challenge yourself and your audience.

Be **Heard**

You may choose to be your own devil's advocate and set out your arguments for and against an idea, only then inviting others to respond.

Get **Noticed**

Communicating your ideas to a broader audience, including externals such as industry professionals and experts, can increase the breadth of your network and help to build your profile.

7
The Great Anti-Glossary

'Hello, I am an *enthusiastic*, *creative* and *highly motivated* individual with *excellent attention to detail*. Along with *extensive experience* in my *field* and a solid *track record*, I regard myself as an *organised, trustworthy, innovative* and *analytical problem solver*, with a *reliable* and *dynamic* approach to projects that require great *communication skills*. I am an *effective team player*, able to work to tight deadlines. I can also *work independently* and demonstrate plenty of *self-initiative* and *self-direction*.'

Sound familiar? There are inevitably qualities in the above description that we all have or aspire to. It is also an example of some of the jargon that we use to describe ourselves in order to improve our employment opportunities and business prospects. However, many of these terms have little meaning without a context. And while these qualities are indeed valuable, they could also apply to almost anyone in almost any industry.

Adjusting the frequency

Many of these terms have become clichés, and, as such, they highlight how important it is to be conscious of generalities when exchanging information with others. Without an application or an example, these attributes do not evidence achievement. So, when you are describing or communicating who you are and/or your field of expertise, watch out for your use (or overuse) of this type of language. (For example, unless mentioned in a quotation, you will not find the word 'unique' used in this book.) You do not want to hinder your chances of success by blending in rather than standing out.

It might surprise you to learn that many common buzzwords appear in a large proportion of professional profiles. LinkedIn publishes their top ten overused professional buzzwords, running a complex analysis of millions of users worldwide.[1] The most used word in 2013 was 'responsible',

1. See C. Choi, 'Top 10 Overused LinkedIn Profile Buzzwords of 2013' [infographic], *LinkedIn Blog* (11 December 2013). Available at: http://blog.linkedin.com/2013/12/11/buzzwords-2013/

followed by 'strategic', 'creative', 'effective', 'patient' and 'expert'. An infographic also pinpoints where on the globe these terms are being used the most, with 'responsible' being adopted most in, among others, North America, the UK, Saudi Arabia and Singapore. The most overused term in UK profiles was 'enthusiastic'.

It adds little value to include such terms in your profile without providing a context in which the attributes are evidenced, along with further comment and reflection.

Reading the big print

Rather than being words designed to set us apart, many of these terms are simply what you would expect from *any* suitable candidate. You certainly would not apply for a role or connect with a business prospect if you felt you didn't possess these qualities. However, the onus is not just on individuals to seek out work opportunities or connect via social media platforms. Recruiters also have a responsibility to weed out the excessive use of these terms in job descriptions.

Job ads are frequently laden with phrases that lead applicants through a mental box-ticking exercise of requirements, often supplemented with terms such 'high proficiency', 'core competencies', 'commitment' and 'self-starter'. As part of the filtering procedure – the 'big print' – these terms certainly have a place in the recruitment process. But in the wrong hands, they can lead to commonalities that make differentiation a challenge.

Using the word 'creative' in a profile for a 'creative person', for instance, is only of benefit if you can demonstrate how and where you have been able to solve problems and meet challenges. It involves going beyond adjectives towards more demonstrative and descriptive accounts of your applied expertise. On the other hand, soft skills (i.e. non-technical skills or interpersonal skills) provide a gateway by which you can really start to differentiate yourself.[2] However, use a rigorous level of definition to distinguish yourself from other people who are using the same terms. This can be supported by either personal or professional experience that will define you and build in your distinctiveness.

Businesses, too, are not exempt from the inclination to inject frequently used words that, while probably true, resonate little with their audience if used to excess. How many organisations do you know of that operate with an 'ethos of excellence', 'best practice' and 'competence'? Unless words like these are used in context, there is a danger that the creative and emotional areas of the brain (the frontal cortex) become desensitised and less responsive to clichés and metaphors.[3]

Getting under the bonnet

Breaking away from the myriad of buzzwords to find distinctive descriptors or indicators that set you apart may require a fresh outlook. Set aside some time to reappraise and re-evaluate your attributes:

- Stop and question what some of these 'must-have' terms really mean and whether they are a good fit for your experience.

- Consider if the terms are simply verbal fillers, particularly if you can't provide a context where they can be demonstrated. What other qualities do you have that you can talk up instead?

- Apply simplicity when filtering out linguistic demons – if anything you say demonstrates a lack of creative thinking, then get rid of it.

When all is said and done, at the end of the day, it's best to avoid clichés like the plague!

2. In *Promote Yourself: The New Rules for Building an Outstanding Career* (London: Piatkus, 2013), Dan Schawbel discusses the importance of soft skills and interpersonal skills. He compiled a list of skills that managers of Fortune 500 companies believe young employees need in order to progress in their careers. The list includes a strong work ethic, optimistic/positive attitude, good communication skills and time management abilities, among many more.

3. E. R. Cardillo and colleagues established that clichés and metaphors tend to be received as predictable, ordinary and mainstream. They found that there was less brain activity in comparison to when the brain received original metaphors and phrases. See E. R. Cardillo, C. E. Watson, G. L. Schmidt, A. Kranjec and A. Chatterjee, 'From Novel to Familiar: Tuning the Brain for Metaphors, *Neuroimage* 59(4) (2012): 3212–3221. Available at: http://www.ncbi.nlm.nih.gov/pmc/articles/PMC3288556/.

Shift gear: write the talk

Consider the scenario of meeting someone for the first time and describing to them what you do for a living or a project you are working on. Depending on the nature of your work or expertise, this may come very naturally to you within the regular flow of conversation. Now refer back to the overused words at the start of this chapter. What is the likelihood that you would use any of those words in a verbal conversation about who you are or what you do? It would be unconventional (and possibly a bit weird) to actually hear someone describe themselves as 'dynamic', 'reliable' or a 'great team player with excellent communication skills' during a normal conversation. Instead, we adopt a more informal and natural tone. So, while your personal profile should not be overly informal, you should select your words intelligently and, at the same time, be very mindful of what the competition might be saying.[4]

4. Robert Boduch describes the importance of considering the competition: 'Your competition is everywhere ... all vying for your prospect's time and attention. Your challenge is to cut through the clutter with an offer that's pertinent, in demand and irresistibly appealing.' R. Boduch, *Online Copywriting Secrets: 170+ Quick Tips for Making All Your Web Sales Copy More Compelling, Convincing and Responsive* (Kindle edition, n.d.), loc. 56.

Remember

Develop an acute awareness of the way in which you describe yourself, your business or your projects. If using generic terms, ensure that you understand the true meaning, consider carefully how frequently you use them and apply personal relevance and context from your own expertise and experience.

Be **Seen**

Consider how the overuse of certain terms might make you invisible; they are inevitably being used by your competition too.

Be **Heard**

Ensure that your profile communicates and augments your experiences so that you are heard beyond the common rhetoric.

Get **Noticed**

Think about how context and applied examples will get you noticed so that you are adding a further dimension to your description.

8
Know More Than Your Onions

How much do you know about your industry either from a historical, present-day or future perspective? Regardless of your profession, having a sound understanding of your sector is fundamental in an environment where knowledge and insight are powerful commodities. It is vital to build up knowledge about organisations, market share, positioning, competition, trends, technological and social advancements and ongoing developments in order to gain advantage and maximise your business opportunities and prospects.

Knowledge acquisition increases not only the depth of your familiarity with the sector but also the bandwidth within which you can make informed choices about the kinds of organisations you want to work with in the future. And being able to demonstrate this intelligence will further communicate your awareness and enthusiasm. Industry expertise and vision give you an advantage over your competitors as you are demonstrating that you have the knowledge, resources and contacts to progress and make well-informed decisions.[1]

Scientia est potentia

Commonly attributed to Sir Frances Bacon, '*scientia est potentia*' roughly translates as 'knowledge is power' or 'the potential of knowledge creates power'.[2] Knowledge is powerful collateral; it can really start to create differentiation boundaries. It is therefore important that our knowledge is communicated and that it creates and sustains connections. Remember that the acquisition of knowledge, both inside and outside your area of expertise, is a gateway to new opportunities.[3] Staying within your knowledge comfort zone may limit your capacity to venture into uncharted territory and, furthermore, inhibit the formation of constructive alliances.

1. Glenn Llopis talks about 'circular vision' – connecting with available resources at every opportunity. See G. Llopis, *Earning Serendipity: Four Skills for Creating and Sustaining Good Fortune in Your Work* (Austin, TX: Greenleaf Book Group, 2009).

2. In their book, *Experts: The Knowledge and Power of Expertise* (Abingdon: Routledge, 2011), Nico Stehr and Reiner Grundmann observe that the term *potentia* (capacity) denotes 'the power of knowledge ... Knowledge is not power in the usual sense of the word power, but rather potential power' (p. 3).

3. Stehr and Grundmann describe knowledge as a capacity to act: 'Knowledge is discovery. Newly discovered knowledge expands our opportunities to take action' (*ibid.*, p. 2).

Knowing your fruit and veg

Meet Stuart. Stuart is a greengrocer running a family business in his local market. He is highly knowledgeable about fruit and vegetables – from country of origin to how to cook them. As well as his almost encyclopaedic knowledge, he has to be aware of seasonal variations, consumer demands, market trends and patterns. He is also very aware of the impact that larger players, such as the big four supermarkets, have had on his business in recent years. However, he has devised strategies to ensure that he creates value for his customers and has developed distinctive elements in his business that set him apart from his competitors.

In addition, he is attentive to changing consumer behaviour in an environment where convenience means that some of his customers need to shop in one place and have no time for that 'special purchase'. He also has to be highly sensitive to factors that are invisible to his customers, such as changes in footfall, location and relationships with stakeholders (e.g. farmers). All these elements have a profound impact on pricing – keeping costs competitive and in line with (or better than) those of his competitors.

Stuart has been able to respond to the growth and interest in organic produce and has made this one of his selling points. He also supplies products that are harder to obtain in supermarkets alongside specialist knowledge about that produce. He is well-informed about many other factors that, indirectly, could have an impact on his company but are largely out of his control, including legislation, politics, social change, technological and agricultural innovation. This ensures that he is relatively up to date with the latest developments that could affect his business.

Stuart has a 360° vision of his products, business and industry, understanding where it has been, where it is now and, more importantly, where it is going. His foresight has set him apart from his competitors – he is staying one step ahead. This level of industry insight provides a lens through which he can make better informed and more intelligent decisions, backed up by relevant facts and figures. Stuart's grasp of 'market intelligence', and his ability to acquire and analyse information in order to understand the market, is a valuable asset to him as well as his customers.

Active industry awareness, like Stuart's, requires the ability to research, understand and interpret important information about your business sector.

Moving with the social times

It is all very well to accumulate knowledge and build industry awareness, but it is equally important to understand that audiences, as well as sectors, are moving targets, so adaptation and reaction to consumer demand is vital. Markets and audiences are not static. Behaviours and trends are affected by multiple factors – for example, technological advancements in social networks have enabled dialogue not only from consumer to business but also from consumer to consumer. Ordinary people now have the power to influence decision making through simple and effective mechanisms, such as star ratings, customer reviews, comments, likes and dislikes.

More than ever, individuals, entrepreneurs and businesses need to be not only part of social media advancement, but also to demonstrate that they are responsive to it. The days of disgruntled consumers writing in green ink to vent their dissatisfaction, only to receive a reply by post a few weeks later, are numbered. With the emergence of social media, email, Twitter and so on, the channels through which we can express our satisfaction/dissatisfaction, or engage in dialogue with brands, is now faster, more accessible, more efficient and more dynamic. As a result, the response times in which brands connect with consumers is decreasing.[4]

Who exactly are 'they'?

While it is obviously important to build up an understanding of your target audience, it can also be argued that, in a fast moving and constantly changing world, the idea of targeting a specific demographic (e.g. age, gender, race) is no longer a sensible way to make informed business decisions or generate growth. If your business model is targeted at an age group of, say, 18 to 25-year-olds, it is possible that many of the age-specific frameworks for that group may become obsolete as they grow older; the business model may not resonate with the new occupants of that age bracket.[5]

So, if the notion of the demographic as one of the factors that you might use to target your market is questionable as a viable indicator, then you need to develop an understanding of how your consumers react to economic or social change, and then adapt to new trends in behaviour and attitude. The recent economic downturn, for instance, has had an impact on how and where we spend our leisure time.

Any research you do, either online or offline, will require you to maintain an investigative mindset. Once you have accumulated the necessary data, don't just sit on it; spend time filtering and extracting the useful information which will provide you with a comprehensive and impressive understanding of your market.

Beyond statistics

Access to information and resources, such as published research information, national market/industry reports, statistics, trends and

4. According to research conducted by Simply Measured, average response times to tweets is 4.4 hours from time of writing (October 2013). See http://www.simplymeasured.com.

5. An article in *Marketing Magazine* highlights the perils of planning against demographics: 'the demographic has come under pressure like never before. Increasingly, segmenting or measuring audiences by common demographics such as age, gender, race, disabilities, mobility, home ownership, employment status and even location are being devalued by the pace of change in the UK population.' See 'Media Starts to Catch Up with the Changing Consumer' (16 October 2012). Available at: http://www.marketingmagazine.co.uk/article/1154781/media-starts-catch-changing-consumer.

analysis, is vital in gaining insights to your informed career or business development. The trade press, as well as blogs and articles, also provides new insights and opinions on emerging themes.[6]

Enhanced sector knowledge will empower you as you extend your industry know-how and work towards becoming an authority in your field. Building up industry knowledge can have a positive impact on your professional development and can set you apart from your competitors. Expressing a critical viewpoint as an expert means you will become respected for your industry insight, thus building professional credibility.[7]

Knowledge in new cultural sectors

Knowledge beyond your field of expertise is crucial and will extend potential opportunities for collaboration and future work prospects. Whether geographical, organisational or by sector, it is important to develop your understanding of unfamiliar cultures when entering new markets. When a brand (or product) considers entering a new market in a new geographical location, it needs to consider not only the nuances and details of the industry but also any cultural or ethnic sensitivities. This requires more than just professional knowledge; individuals and organisations must recognise the significance of bridging cultural gaps.[8]

6. The Office for National Statistics provides some of the most up-to-date economic, social and business information: http://www.statistics.gov.uk.

7. In her article, 'Want to Become Known As An Industry Expert?', Cari Sommer describes the importance of being confident as an 'expert': 'If you feel confident enough to put your name out there and speak about a particular market segment of industry, feel confident enough to tell people that you're doing so.' C. Sommer, 'Want to Become Known as an Industry Expert? 3 Tips to Get You Started', Forbes (18 January 2012). Available at: http://www.forbes.com/sites/carisommer/2012/01/18/want-to-become-known-as-an-industry-expert-3-tips-to-get-you-started/.

8. Gary Locke and Frank Gavin observe: 'Understanding cultural difference can help us develop the patience and congeniality necessary to undertake successful business projects. The person without a cultural understanding may look at a foreign development with disdain or fear. The person with an appreciation for culture tends to look at new issues with curiosity and respect.' G. Locke and F. Gavin, *Export: Five Keys to Entering New Markets* (Singapore: John Wiley & Sons, 2011), p. 199.

Remember

Knowledge is power. The more you can demonstrate your expertise by researching your industry, the greater your advantage over your rivals. It will also increase your networks and opportunities. Understand and utilise the full potential of resources that can enhance your knowledge. Consider how you can make these resources work for you so that they become important tools in differentiating you from your competitors.

Be **Seen**

Increasing your knowledge (and in some cases, cultural awareness) will contribute to defining you and your objectives.

Be **Heard**

Advanced sector knowledge has the ability to give you an advantage over rivals as well as raising your profile and increasing your prospects of being heard as an authority in your field.

Get **Noticed**

New knowledge should not just be acquired and accumulated; it should also be acted upon. This can get you noticed by potential audiences, old or new.

9
Many See –
Fewer Notice

Visionaries and leading business people are often credited with the ability to see or plan for the future, entering uncharted landscapes and realising ideas where others have feared to go. But this skill is not only reserved for celebrated entrepreneurs; it is something we must all do at various stages in our careers. It is imperative that you detect any gaps that will enable you to make the most out of market opportunities ahead of your competitors.

It is also beneficial to be able to locate changes or shifts in the current landscape and to act swiftly. A vital attribute of any change-maker is to be open to change and to make effective decisions across the enterprise.[1] Developing an outlook that enables you to notice opportunities requires a forward-thinking mindset that:

- Fosters elements of risk taking, courage and unpredictability that you might normally associate with entrepreneurs or individuals with innovative ideas.

- Demands high levels of curiosity and an investigative nature.

- Builds the ability to make astute connections – some of the greatest discoveries evolved from relatively unconnected factors that came to bear fruit only with shrewd vision.

- Creates capacity to see potential in the smallest of opportunities and, more importantly, the ability to convert them into possibilities.

Judging a book by its customer – no regrets

The ability to see what others don't, or going beyond the predictable, requires sensitivity to the past, present and future. It also requires a sophisticated talent for analysing research findings and data in order to inform important decisions. Furthermore, it means being highly perceptive to what people are saying, writing and reading about; what

1. Vincent P. Barabba's book, *The Decision Loom*, explores strategies to ensure that companies adopt market intelligence wisely, including having an enterprise mindset that is open to change, thinking and acting holistically, being able to adapt the business design to changing conditions and making decisions interactively using a variety of methods. See V. P. Barabba, *The Decision Loom: A Design for Interactive Decision-Making in Organizations* (Axminster: Triarchy Press, 2011).

they are doing and when they are doing it. This draws on an amalgam of being curious and seeing big opportunities in even the smallest of niches.

One example is this: Jeff Bezos who, as the founder and CEO of Amazon.com, saw way beyond the remit of the fledgling internet in the early 1990s. With a background in computer science and electrical engineering, he saw the potential of the web as a powerful consumer channel; at the time, it was a framework used mainly by government agencies and academic institutions.

In the early 1990s, when web usage was reportedly growing by almost 2300% per year,[2] Bezos built a vision around dynamic internet growth. His original business model was developed from research gleaned from mail order businesses. Following some extensive investigation, and after making a list of twenty of the best products to sell online, he saw books as an ideal internet product. As he later observed, 'Books are incredibly unusual in one respect, and that is that there are more items in the book category than there are items in any other category by far.'[3] Amazon was born.

Bezos reportedly attributes his early decisions to what he calls the 'regret minimisation framework' – 'looking back on life from its end to imagine the results'.[4] In order to minimise the number of regrets in his life, he fostered a mindset that enabled him to mentally project forward and analyse life decisions at the age of around 80, and then come back to the present day. He says this made certain business decisions incredibly easy for him. It was a strategy that would have a profound impact on his vision to apply courageous thinking and access new markets.

The hidden treasure

Let's take the job market as an example and the assertion that '80% of jobs aren't advertised'. This fact (if, indeed, it is fact) highlights the importance of networking, building connections, being curious, striking

2. See Glenn Llopis, 'What We Can All Learn From Amazon about Seeing Business Opportunities Others Don't See', *Forbes* (7 February 2011). Available at: http://www.forbes.com/sites/glennllopis/2011/02/07/what-we-can-all-learn-from-amazon-about-seeing-business-opportunities-others-dont-see/.

3. Quoted in S. Wasserman, 'The Amazon Effect', *The Nation* (18 June 2012). Available at: http://www.thenation.com/article/168125/amazon-effect#.

4. See Llopis, 'What We Can All Learn from Amazon'.

while the iron *isn't* hot and, more importantly, seeing openings ahead of the pack.

This statement should perhaps be reframed to read, '80% of job opportunities are available'. This alerts us that we should be listening for clues or signs that the majority might not necessarily pick up on before a recruitment campaign goes mainstream – for example, announcements, changes of personnel, news of imminent recruitment drives or rapid business growth. In many cases, this information is available through business blogs, LinkedIn groups, industry news publications and bulletin boards. You just need to know where to look.

The same degree of proactivity also applies to entrepreneurs and businesses who should be looking out for opportunities ahead of the competition.

Catching the early bird

Aim to attract the attention of trendsetters who spot opportunities early. Early adopters are extremely valuable to the process of innovation and are also in the advantageous position of occupying new and untested territory.[5] The early birds (usually one of the first in line in a queue for a new product release, often camping out for days in advance) are crucial in building and maintaining relationships between themselves, brands and later followers.

Change agents, visionaries, design thinkers, products and brands should be sensitive to trendsetters and manage their relationships with them effectively. When early adopters are the first to try out a new operating system – for instance, as part of a pre-launch – it is important that channels of communication are robust and well managed and that any subsequent iteration process is handled efficiently.

Pioneers (i.e. innovators, change agents, imaginative thinkers) of all kinds share common attributes. These include venturing into unknown

5. The term 'early adopter' was originally conceived by Professor of Rural Psychology Everett Rogers. He established five categories or groupings: innovators, early adopters, early majority, late majority and laggards. See E. M. Rogers, *Diffusion of Innovations* (New York: Simon & Schuster, 2003).

territory and testing fertile ground – spaces where the natural order is to defy convention and look for potential in the smallest of opportunities. It is therefore fundamental that you:

- Identify with early adopters by understanding their needs for new ideas.
- Demonstrate the common attributes that connect pioneers and early adopters.
- Listen intently to the reactions of early adopters.
- Stay on the radar within the community of pioneers and early adopters.

Remember

Being able to notice what others do not requires the ability to step outside the remit of the predictable and enter new and sometimes untested ground. This requires risk taking as well as astute judgement. Make sure you understand the demands of early adopters who can be highly instrumental in the development of your ideas.

Be **Seen**

Consider what steps you need to take to ensure that you are visible to early adopters.

Be **Heard**

Pioneering steps are never silent. Announcing breakthroughs and major developments is a vital part of the journey.

Get **Noticed**

Becoming a leading figure in your field will attract collaborators or even competitors. It is vital to sustain your capacity for foresight and forward thinking in order to get ahead and stay ahead.

10
The Small, Mighty and Beautiful

An increasing rise in entrepreneurship and the number of small businesses has changed the economic and enterprise landscape in the UK during the past few years.[1] This growth represents a positive movement in business, commerce and enterprise but, more importantly, it reveals the potential for smaller, leaner and sharper organisations to thrive. The structure of these lighter weight companies means that, more than ever, businesses can operate with more flexible cultures of collaboration, knowledge sharing and communication, shucking off the more rigid restraints of larger corporate entities.

Working with or for smaller companies has also become a more attractive proposition for those of us who are seeking a more dynamic and independent workplace. While the tradition has usually been to work for huge organisations that look great on your CV, there is a growing tendency for people to join small start-ups. The benefits include flexible hours, a creative and innovative atmosphere, diverse work assignments, greater ownership of projects, valuable interpersonal experiences and increased opportunities for growth and advancement.[2]

Co-working minds think alike

Alongside growing numbers of small businesses and start-ups, there has been a significant rise in the number of companies that hire freelance workers.[3] As freelancers have also been on the increase, this has created a demand for more co-working spaces and incubation environments for sharing ideas and collaboration.[4] Users of these spaces have the advantage of a collaborative working environment where they can expand personal and professional networks and grow their businesses or ideas.

The growth in the freelance economy and the increase in co-working spaces has, in turn, created a demand for inspiring and productive workplaces. Users report finding these environments highly supportive, leading to creative collaboration and knowledge sharing.[5]

1. According to statistics released by the Department for Business Innovation & Skills, at the start of 2012 there were an estimated 4.8 million UK private sector businesses; 99.2% of these were small employing 0 to 49 employees. See Department for Business Innovation & Skills, *Business Population Estimates for the UK and Regions 2012* (17 October 2012). Available at: https://www.gov.uk/government/uploads/system/uploads/attachment_data/file/80247/bpe-2012-stats-release-4.pdf.

2. See H. Huhman, '6 Reasons People Leave Big Companies to Join Startups', *Tech Cocktail* (1 June 2013). Available at: http://tech.co/6-reasons-people-leave-big-companies-to-join-startups-2013-06.

3. Katie Jacobs observes that 'payments made to freelancers by businesses have ... gone up by 47% since 2012'. K. Jacobs, 'UK Freelance Economy Booming, Research Finds', *HR Magazine* (23 August 2013). Available at: http://www.hrmagazine.co.uk/hro/news/1078168/uk-freelance-economy-booming-research#sthash.3o4Ppmv6.dpuf.

It is essential for any new enterprise or business to keep the emerging co-working community on their radar, whether or not you are renting desk space. This could be to instigate, facilitate or host an event that would be of interest to the co-working community. This has very obvious rewards, including exposing you to a vast and diverse network, as well as highlighting your service or offering to a dynamic and vibrant grouping. So, it is also important to:

- Consider making yourself known within a community of co-working space members.

- Think about how you can use the co-working environment either as a member or as fertile testing ground for ideas.

- Understand how being within these small environments can put you at the heart and soul of the decision making process.

Reach out – then reach for the stars

While there has been a significant shift towards freelancing and co-working, being employed by the world's largest and most desirable companies still has huge appeal. Not only is it highly attractive in terms of career history, but in many cases the job satisfaction and kudos is also a major draw. In the United States, branding firm Universum surveyed over 60,000 undergraduate students and asked them to name their 'ideal' employers.[6] Predictably, business and IT students ranked Google and Apple high on their list; Walt Disney, Ernst & Young, Deloitte, J. P. Morgan, Nike, PricewaterhouseCoopers, Goldman Sachs and KPMG were among their top ten (although Microsoft was surprisingly missing). Engineering students listed NASA, Boeing and BMW among their top ten.

Human resources departments in these large organisations receive literally thousands of résumés and CVs, dramatically minimising the

4. *Deskmag*, the co-working space magazine, conducted its own study using data from the Global Coworking Survey. This revealed that, as of February 2013, there were around 2,500 co-working spaces globally. This converts to approximately 4.5 new co-working spaces every day throughout the world during the previous year. See C. Foertsch, '4.5 New Coworking Spaces Per Work Day', *Deskmag* (4 March 2013). Available at: http://www.deskmag.com/en/2500-coworking-spaces-4-5-per-day-741.

5. An example is Impact Hub – part innovation lab, part business incubator, part community centre. It is a rapidly expanding global community of co-working spaces with thousands of members and collaborators in numerous locations around the world. For more information visit http://www.impacthub.net.

6. See M. Casserly, 'Dream Companies for the Class of 2012: Everybody Wants to Work at Google', *Forbes* (11 May 2012). Available at: http://www.forbes.com/sites/meghancasserly/2012/05/11/dream-companies-for-class-2012-everybody-wants-to-work-at-google/.

visibility of any one candidate, however outstanding. So, there is a good argument for starting your career with a smaller organisation where you can stand out more effectively in a less saturated environment.

Regardless of the increased growth in co-working and the desirability of working for smaller companies, many of us still regard small firms as a stepping stone to larger and more well-known companies – that is, as a gateway to bigger success. This is unfortunate. While regular and consistent career progression can be great, there are many benefits to embracing the spirit of small and medium-sized organisations that can foster valuable skills and personal growth. To expand your reach, perhaps you need to think big but focus on the small.

Small start – massive potential

Not so long ago, if a budding musician or artist wanted to get a record contract and get signed, they would almost certainly have had to prepare a demo cassette tape or CD with a few tracks to give the A&R people an idea of their talent and music style. The demo would then get shipped off to record companies, which in many cases would place it on top of an ever-increasing heap of other hopefuls' tapes or CDs. You may have heard of romantic stories of artists who sent in a demo to a record label, which was won over by their brilliance and then invited the artist in for a meeting to discuss a recording deal. A short while later, the artist would ceremoniously hold a fountain pen over a contract guaranteeing them riches beyond their wildest dreams.

Today, it is virtually unheard of for an artist to get signed by a large label on the premise of a demo. Aspiring artists now need to be multifaceted, multichannelled and multitasking machines adept at self-promotion and marketing *before* they get anywhere near a record company. Bands have always turned to live performances to build up a following, but the internet now offers an excellent way to demonstrate their artistry. From live showcases and gigs to online spaces, such as YouTube channels, it has become essential for performers to build a strong platform, develop networks and generate a loyal fan base.

Musicians must expand their connectivity to ensure that their remit transcends the music industry per se; if they start causing a social media stir they might just attract the right decision makers in the industry. The more web-savvy have seen digital platforms, such as YouTube and Vimeo, not simply as video hosting and sharing sites, but as social networking and social connecting sites in an arena rich with A&R and talent scouts.

As with musicians, so it is for the rest of us. It is important for *all* new enterprises to understand the power of the various digital mediums available and of their potential to increase audience size.

As more of us engage with visual content, regardless of our industry, it has become a fundamental skill to be able to create and curate visually arresting and interesting content in order to make us or our product desirable, believable and attractive to new audiences. This, in turn, builds potential for growth and connectivity, while simultaneously communicating our distinctiveness.[7]

It is also beneficial to explore the potential of small communities in order to mine the discourse and engagement for new dimensions to your projects. However, although small communities and enterprises have power, it is connected eco-systems that have the real potential to expand connectivity.

7. Ekaterina Walter highlights the growing trend for brands to use visual content as an effective online communication tool, observing, 'When it comes to their products, businesses are learning to show, not tell.' E. Walter, 'The Rise of Social Media', *Fast Company* (28 August 2012). Available at: http://www.fastcompany.com/3000794/rise-visual-social-media.

Remember

While thinking big in terms of organisations, it is helpful to remember the many benefits of working and collaborating with smaller enterprises. Co-working spaces are dynamic environments; as well as being a member, you can also use these spaces as testing fields and incubators for ideas.

Be **Seen**

You and your ideas are more visible within smaller enterprises, which also provide a platform for open discourse and development.

Be **Heard**

You can explore how testing your ideas (through talks, workshops or events) can boost your profile but also contribute to your research.

Get **Noticed**

Getting yourself known within small organisations and co-working spaces is bound to get you noticed as you will be in touch with key individuals and decision makers.

11

[n=e]=CE – Achieving the Balance

Intriguing equation. All will be revealed shortly.

With the increase in social media and social networks, along with the rapid accumulation of so-called friends, contacts and likes, have we lost the meaning and importance of connectivity as a vital factor in building and sustaining relationships in our personal and professional lives?

Arguably, being part of a large or varied network does not necessarily constitute a well-connected individual or group. On the contrary, it may demonstrate our ability to do just that: make contact and create networks. But how active are those networks? Do they play a key role in the development of opportunities? Once you have built a network, creating ongoing experiences is equally fundamental.

In this chapter, we will focus on the relationship between experiences and networks in the context of forging meaningful connections to progress business, career or personal opportunities.

Connecting eye to eye

Being able to connect – building networks and experiences – is essential when developing relationships with your audience. Increasingly, 'content marketing' is being adopted as a strategy to connect brands and engage customers.[1] Brands that are producing meaningful and 'brand relevant' content on their websites and blogs are able to generate better customer loyalty. There is good evidence that online content marketing offers great opportunities for consumers to engage with your brand via TV, radio or press ads.[2]

It is clear to see why brands might focus on generating content that is not necessarily a hard sell if any genuinely enjoyable content is in the interest of the consumer. It is therefore becoming more and more important for individuals and/or groups to generate content across various streams that can provide transparent and meaningful access to

1. Destiny Bennett describes the increased use of content marketing by companies as a way to engage with their audience by 'setting out to entertain readers or viewers, and evoke a sense of "likeability" toward the brand'. D. Bennett, 'Content Marketing Connects Brands with Target Audiences', *American Genius* (28 March 2013). Available at: http://agbeat.com/business-marketing/content-marketing-connects-brands-with-target-audiences/.

2. Bennett goes on to say: 'if a consumer likes your brand and regularly comes to your content portals to read blogs, watch videos or interact with some other form of branded content and entertainment that you provide ... they then make a positive association with your brand and will come back on a regular basis to see what's new' (ibid.).

the brand. This also creates a communication channel from which it is possible to connect with audiences and demonstrate knowledge and leadership in their field.

In the rest of this chapter, we will explore some of the components of connectivity that are fundamental to personal, career and professional development, focusing primarily on networks and experiences.

If the expansion of your Luck Surface Area (see Chapter 2) is the combined activity of doing and telling, and this can increase the spectrum of opportunity, it would be wrong to assume that just having an extensive network of friends (even if it is 150 individuals) constitutes effective connectivity. You may be networked and 'in contact', but to what degree are you really *connected*?

Connectivity – the experience factor

We need to take into account another factor which is an integral element of connectivity – experiences. Within the context of connectivity, experience is the frame-holder under which a vast array of components contribute to building meaningful connections. These include environment, culture, literature, food, fashion, media, politics, commerce, economics, technology and many more. Our accumulation of experiences (not just networks and community) forms an effective gateway to fostering connectivity and common ground with groups and individuals.

But is it enough to accumulate experiences without making the most of networks? Or vice versa, immersing in vibrant networks but not really being mindful or capitalising on experiences? It might require a combination of the two in what I would refer to as 'connectivity rebalance'.

[n=e]=CE unmasked

A big network does not necessarily constitute an active network; it could actually be underactive. It is possible that someone might be a very active networker, accumulating lots of contacts but not always following them through. A typical individual who has a vast yet dormant network is also likely to have a high number of contacts in their online social networks (e.g. 500+ LinkedIn connections) and a relatively large list of email contacts, although will not have been in contact with the majority of these for a long time.

On the other hand, an individual who has a broad spectrum of experiences, encounters and environments – for example, through travel or cultural experiences – could arguably have a fairly small network. An example might be an individual who has had a high turnaround of jobs and roles in various companies, sectors or even countries. However, as varied and colourful as their professional history and experience is, they may have only a relatively small or limited active network.

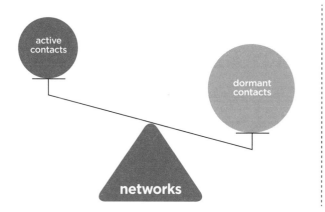

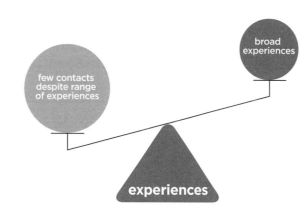

Connectivity equilibrium requires a balance and awareness of networks and experiences. So, [n=e]=CE simply means that connectivity equilibrium is achieved through a balance of active networks (n) and experiences (e), from which you can forge active contacts. By being open to new experiences you can develop and sustain networks; conversely, by capitalising on active networks you can build new experiences.

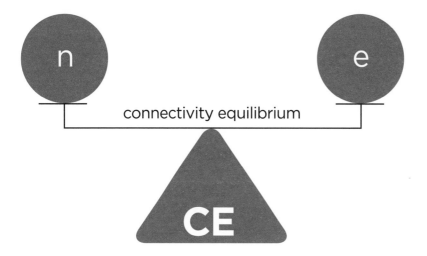

Consider where you sit within these two scenarios. Are there any imbalances that you need to address?

[n=e]=CE is just a working hypothesis and is not a measurable factor – that is, you cannot have a high connectivity equilibrium score in the same way as you would for an IQ test or psychometric test. However, the patterns are very real, as is the importance of creating a balanced interrelation between networks and experiences.

Connecting with your environment

The space in which we think, work, create, design and innovate is an important bridge from the imagination to the application and implementation of our ideas. In some cases, the environment in which we create becomes the hallmark of our creative process. But in order to accomplish this, and generate the best output, we need to be able to connect fully with our environment.

For hundreds of years, artists, creatives, inventors and scientists have become in tune with their creative process by connecting with their environments. J. K. Rowling famously wrote in cafes in her early days as a budding author, Ernest Hemingway reportedly wrote while standing up and Marcel Proust seldom emerged from the cork-lined room in which he wrote many of his novels.

By stimulating our senses we can enhance the creative process.[3] It would be interesting to discover how different environments could impact positively on your productivity. For example, you could experiment by working in a public space where the combination of smell, audio and visuals might conjure up new insights, thoughts and inspiration.[4]

3. Sally Augustin observes that scientists have learned that 'Cinnamon-vanilla smells and creativity seem to be linked'. S Augustin, 'The Smell is Right – Using Scents to Enhance Life', *Psychology Today* (23 December 2009). Available at: http://www.psychologytoday.com/blog/people-places-and-things/200912/the-smell-is-right-using-scents-enhance-life.

4. Alexandra Enders has explored the environmental stimuli of various writers, focusing on a combination of spatial, object and time elements: 'Each writer needs to establish the configurations of this creative space, which incorporates memory, imagination, intention, and curiosity.' A. Enders, 'The Importance of Place: Where Writers Write and Why', *Poets & Writers* (March/April 2008). Available at: http://www.pw.org/content/importance_place_where_writers_write_and_why_0?cmnt_all=1.

Remember

The connectivity equilibrium, [n=e]=CE, is achieved through a balance and awareness of active networks and experiences. Keep the concept in mind and constantly review where you fit within the spectrum. It is important to achieve a balance of both in order to ensure that neither element becomes inactive or transient. It is also crucial that, once a balance is achieved, they are informing each other.

Be **Seen**

You may very well have an impressive CV of experiences. It is therefore important to take care that you are also increasing your visibility through these experiences, thus building your networks.

Be **Heard**

Having a large number of connections in your social media networks is no guarantee of being heard if you are not also augmenting who you are and what you do.

Get **Noticed**

While reactivating dormant networks and contacts, create a focus on getting noticed and developing contacts through a broad range of experiences.

12
The Creative Paradox

Good ideas are great. But unfortunately that is where many of them stay; without concrete plans to implement them they remain as good ideas. It is fairly easy to come up with proposals, but less so to follow through with action.[1] When we generate ideas for our career or business, we need to understand that, while creativity and ideation may be abundant, the definite outcomes we wish for are harder to achieve.

Consequently, it can be helpful to think more critically about creativity – and its hazards – and how new insights can genuinely contribute to bringing about material distinctiveness in your business, professional or personal life. The following statements are presented as opening salvos to open up a fresh debate on creativity and its role in defining your objectives.

Creative idea generation requires boundaries ... and a deadline

Even though we might choose to adopt a free or lateral thinking approach to problem solving, ideas require a framework within which to operate. This is not to say that creative ideas should be hampered by overly restrictive rules or structures, but it is reasonable to propose (realistic) cut-off points for evaluation and reflection before carefully planning forward.

Whether you are adhering to short or long deadlines, consider how the time allotted could enhance or detract from the development of your creative ideas. Within a given time frame, you should aim to establish open and closed modes of productivity – that is, when it is best to be in an open mode (i.e. taking a wide-angled view of the problem) or a closed mode (i.e. requiring a zooming in and focus on implementation).[2]

1. Scott Belsky comments on the perils of ideation: 'A surplus of ideas is as dangerous as a drought. The tendency to jump from idea to idea to idea spreads your energy horizontally rather than vertically. As a result you'll struggle to make progress' (Belsky, *Making Ideas Happen*, p. 31).

2. The actor and comedian John Cleese produced a training video for Video Arts in which he describes two key modes of thinking that contribute to the creative process – open and closed modes. He says: 'We need to be in the open mode when pondering a problem ... once we come up with a solution, we must then switch to the closed mode to implement it. To be at our most efficient, we need to be able to switch backwards and forward between the two modes ... too often we get stuck in the closed mode.' Available (for a fee) at: http://www.videoarts. com/Vintage-Video-Arts/ the-john-cleese-files/.

Creative ideas are stepping stones – not the destination

Avoiding failure and constantly pursuing the right answer can create a blind spot in which future opportunities are compromised.[3] In the spirit of embracing 'failed' concepts, ideas should be seen as stepping stones to another idea and as part of a longer iterative process. Being creative is often cyclical – we may very well revisit a well-trodden stone in order to reassess or review a situation.

Try to adopt a progressive and experimental mindset so that you can actually get going on a project, no matter how embryonic. This might involve making bold steps to take forward a concept that isn't necessarily finished or is still a work in progress. You may also need to accommodate feedback from others (including devil's advocates) and make room for unforeseen developments. Perhaps adopt beta mode or lab thinking to progress through these formative stages.

It is so tempting to be focused purely on solutions, but we should not resist the evolutionary transformation of ideas.

Creative ideas may not always be pioneering or innovative

It is important to make the distinction between creative ideas and pioneering innovation, although the two sometimes meet. Creativity carries with it preconditions of originality, expression and vision. In contrast, innovation can be more closely linked with the ability to see the unseen and meet unmet needs.

For example, it is common knowledge that Apple did not 'originally' invent the mobile phone or music player, Dyson did not invent the vacuum cleaner, Amazon was not the first company to get books

3. In *PO: Beyond Yes and No*, Edward de Bono describes what he calls 'intermediate impossibles'. He suggests that we look into the value and virtue of ideas and concepts for longer, relaxing our assumptions by deliberately working with 'absurd' connections. See E. de Bono, *PO: Beyond Yes and No* (Harmondsworth: Penguin, 1990).

delivered to your door and Google was not the first search engine. Yet we associate their products or services with their perceived value as pioneers, visionaries and market leaders. While numerous factors, including brand value and perception, heritage, marketing and communication, played a huge part in the success of these brands, perhaps one commonality is that they all recognised unmet needs and saw opportunities to capitalise on and improve already existing concepts, products or services.

As you embark on new projects, employment or business opportunities, you too need to consider the implications of being pioneering – what it means and whether what you have truly leads the way by being among the first of a kind.

Stuart adds a new spin to his business

You might recall Stuart, the greengrocer from Chapter 8. Although he has vast knowledge about his sector, he operates in an industry that is filled with increasingly knowledgeable and competitive rivals. At weekends, when he books a plot at a local market, he knows that just knowing his onions is not enough to generate queues and build a loyal customer base.

Stuart recognises that he needs to be creative in his approach to connecting with the public. He even knows that undercutting his rivals could result in fruitless price wars. Instead, he does something quite out of the ordinary. He raises his prices to further reflect the quality of his product. But even that was not his key innovation.

He comes up with an idea of 'free' local master classes to share his knowledge, including advice and information about the source and origin of fruit and veg, as well as teaching local children about the benefits of fresh, home-grown food. This not only makes him an authority in his field but it also raises his local profile and enables him to create a distinctive reputation for his business and brand.

There is nothing new in master classes and knowledge sharing, but the application of these strategies to Stuart's enterprise was an effective business decision that served him well. Consider what 'external' methods you can apply to your idea or business to enable you to stand out effectively from your competitors.

Creative ideas are not sufficient

The application of creative ideas is a complex business and is often underestimated. Simply having creative ideas is a long way away from executing them successfully. This requires advanced management skills, the synergy of key individuals, a creative team and an in-depth awareness of practical issues.

While creativity is commonly perceived as the capacity to produce ideas and concepts, this can sometimes be destructive to businesses which 'confuse creativity in the abstract with practical innovation'.[4] Creativity and innovation are not synonyms. They may same share the same objectives, but while ideation is copious, implementation is more scarce.[5]

Creative ideas and implementation are not the domain of one

As you embark on your own plans, consider how the introduction of key individuals or groups might complement or enhance your objectives. You might have the creative vision, but do you have the critical (or logistical) angle to be able to realise your idea? Partnering or collaborating with someone who has a more pragmatic viewpoint could be of enormous benefit. Or it could be that you are the pragmatist and a creative injection would progress your objectives. Alternatively, you

4. Theodore Levitt, Professor of Marketing at Harvard Business School, claims that 'creative people often pass off on others the responsibility for getting down to brass tacks. They have plenty of ideas but little businesslike follow-through ... Many people who are full of ideas simply do not understand how an organization must operate in order to get things done.' T. Levitt, 'Creativity is Not Enough', *Harvard Business Review* (2002). Available at: http://hbr.org/2002/08/creativity-is-not-enough/ar/1.

5. 'The scarce people are those who have the know-how, energy, daring, and staying power to implement ideas' (ibid.).

might need a 'hybrid' to navigate between the creative ideas generator and the pragmatic thinker.[6]

Collaboration between the various character profiles and groupings can have a very positive effect on the creative process and the logistical implementation of ideas and concepts. Fundamentally, all parties should retain clear goals and share the same seamless objectives, rather than remain in their disparate areas with rigid boundaries.

[6]. Scott Belsky offers some interesting perspectives on the profiles of individuals, groups and businesses working on creative projects. For him, 'dreamers', 'doers' and 'incrementalists' all play a key role in the development of a new product, service or business venture (see Belsky, *Making Ideas Happen*, p. 112).

Remember

Creative ideas are an important part of any process. Equally important, though, is the ability to implement them. It is essential to make clear distinctions between ideation and pioneering concepts that meet unmet needs.

Be **Seen**

Identify with ideas not just because they are creative but because they raise attention due to their pioneering or innovative potential.

Be **Heard**

Understanding that creative ideas are contributory factors, rather than a destination, will open up the space necessary to collaborate and share ideas with like-minded groups or individuals.

Get **Noticed**

Consider how you can apply creative ideas to your business that will get you noticed by customers and competitors. It could be the amalgam of two disparate areas that you can exploit in style.

13
Time to Give Up

Whether you are an entrepreneur starting out in business or going for a particular role, promotion or change in your career, you will understand the requirement to make sacrifices in the service of a trade-off to achieving a goal that will reap greater rewards in the future. This might involve renegotiating the time you spend with your family or on socialising, home comforts, leisure time or personal assets and finances. In order to progress in your career, some sacrifices are inevitable, but maintaining a balance is vital.

In this chapter, we are going to explore 'time to give up' from two vantage points: (1) forgoing in order to provide focus, clarity and defined judgement on your objective, and (2) as a valuable currency in making associations and forging new relationships.

Time: perception and finding a balance

Equilibrium in your business and personal life is fundamental in helping you to commit to your career goals. It calls on an inner judgement that is sensitive to needs at both ends of the spectrum – your ambitions at one end and your close support network at the other. You should be 'checking in' with those closest to you for reassurance that you are still on planet earth (unless, of course, your ambition is to be a space engineer or rocket scientist!). However, you also need to be aware of the needs of business associates, colleagues or collaborators.

Time (i.e. clock time) is one of the laws of nature: we cannot change it. However, the psychological perception of time is very much in the domain of the individual. So, arguably, our personal experience of time can be altered. For example, the perception of time of someone working in a 9 to 5 job could be very different to someone starting their own business or working on a personal project. Individuals who might be doing both, by way of having their day job followed by an evening of working on their own business idea, may experience dramatic shifts in their awareness of time.

Carmen's watch

Carmen lives in two time zones. She is an in-house graphic designer working for a television production company. Although she has a lot of creative freedom and a very supportive team and network, she still has to work to extremely tight deadlines and is in demand in many areas of the business. For efficiency and time management purposes, Carmen's creative output is recorded so she has to estimate roughly how much time she has spent on each project. She loves her job but the systematic time management seems to make her days appear longer. She is conscious of every minute and every hour because time is money – and every hour is accountable financially as she is internally 'billing' each department.

Outside of her day job, Carmen has always dreamed of developing her skills as a painter and sculptor and hopes to exhibit and sell her work in the future. As an artist, Carmen is involved in a few personal projects in her spare time. In the evening, she paints and produces work that is not time centric. She is not governed by the clock, but instead by her creativity and freedom. In this 'timeless' space, there are no minutes, no hours, no days. She operates in a totally different mindset.

Carmen is able to think longer term about how she will develop her art. Eventually, she may indeed face deadlines, whether as a result of commissioned work or her own personal targets. But for the short term this is not an issue. Regardless of being in a timeless zone, Carmen is still highly conscious of time; she respects it as a precious commodity and wastes little of it.

If you are operating in different 'time zones', like Carmen, make sure that you are constantly re-evaluating the time you spend on different areas of your personal or professional life. This will help you to make the most out of the time available to develop your ideas and realise your ambitions.

The 'small' big pay-off

Being rooted to your purpose is a crucial factor in maintaining your vision and integrity. This will, no doubt, mean making certain sacrifices or choices that, on the surface, may appear to minimise your potential for greater market share, but conversely may yield greater long-term rewards, such as being a market leader in a specified area. Smaller businesses, particularly those which specialise or provide niche services, are more likely to be able to define a target audience rather than operate in a saturated market.[1]

This is a clear example of sticking with a brand vision: maintaining what you stand for in order to focus more intently on your objective. However, individuals or groups who operate or do business in specialist, niche or select markets are, to some degree, trading off a potentially larger market share in exchange for maintaining the essence of their brand and operating in much smaller, well-defined markets. Many artists, creatives and musicians initially opt to work with smaller 'independent' outfits, or become independent themselves, to retain as much creative freedom and autonomy as possible.[2]

A new perspective on time

In the abstract but highly entertaining film, *In Time* (2011), starring Justin Timberlake, writer and film director Andrew Niccol takes us on a journey. He tells the story of a place where time is the only currency. It is a world where everyone over the age of 25 pays for their own continued existence by earning 'minutes'. Instead of being paid a wage, in the monetary sense, people are remunerated with a longer life. In this world, assets, products and services all cost time (so, for instance, a drink costs around six minutes and a commute on the bus costs around twenty minutes) which is debited from your 'life timeline'.

1. Adam Morgan identifies the characteristics of smaller challenger brands and how they can challenge market leaders. He outlines eight key beliefs or 'credos of successful brands', one of which is 'sacrifice'. He says, 'the ability to sacrifice and concentrate one's focus, voices, and actions more narrowly is one of the few advantages a Challenger has'. A. Morgan, *Eating the Big Fish: How Challenger Brands Can Compete Against Brand Leaders* (2nd edn) (Hoboken, NJ: John Wiley & Sons, 2009), p. 156.

2. For example, Radiohead released their ground-breaking album *In Rainbows* in 2007, their first release since breaking with long-time label EMI. It was available as a CD with a smaller label, but not before it was initially available via a pay-any-price model on the internet. See J. Tyrangiel, 'Radiohead Says: "Pay What You Want"', *Time* (1 October 2007). Available at: http://content.time.com/time/arts/article/0,8599,1666973,00.html#ixzz2igAxTLc1.

As unbelievable and out of this world as the concept may seem, it unpacks some interesting perspectives on the concept of time as a tangible and precious resource, as a commodity and an asset. In the film, individuals are also able to transfer time to each other, highlighting the value of 'giving time' and 'giving up time'. One of the most memorable lines from the film, 'Don't waste my time', comes from a mysterious benefactor who transfers a century of time to Timberlake's character who suddenly becomes 'time wealthy'.

In reality, the clock does not discriminate whether you are time rich or time poor, but it is important to be aware of the nuances of your attitude to time and to make the most out of the opportunities you have. There are many people who wish there were more hours in the day to pursue their dreams and ambitions, but are constrained by either full-time employment or other commitments. As more of us opt to take up fractional roles or flexible working hours, more of us will come to appreciate and make the most of the time and resources available to us outside our existing jobs or commitments.[3]

The value of your time in building new relationships

It is important to consider time in relation to three key factors: networks, currency and value:

1. Networks – when starting out in business or forging a new career path, expanding your existing networks and associations can require a significant amount of investment of your personal time and commitment to generate interest and demand.

2. Currency – it can be helpful to regard your time as a currency from which you can generate, manage and negotiate new associations.

3. See B. Groom, 'Homeworker Numbers Rise 13% in Five Years, Despite Recession', *ft.com* (17 May 2013). Available at: http://www.ft.com/cms/s/0/8411e8a4-be2b-11e2-9b27-00144feab7de.html#ixzz2Tf3eD5VD.

3. Value – it is important that you value your 'free time' and that any contribution you make is valued, acknowledged and not taken for granted.[4]

Giving your time as a valuable commodity is an effective way to define you and, in turn, improve your career prospects. This does not in any way constitute 'free labour', but instead should be a mutual agreement. In the long term, it could also turn out to be an investment that reaps rewards and recognition.

Naturally, when embarking on a new career opportunity, you have a certain amount of leverage in terms of how willing you might be to share or provide your expertise for no payment. But this must always work within a perimeter fence, so that you are not on an endless road of giving away work for nothing.

You may come across individuals or groups who self-market themselves with no intention of earning anything for the foreseeable future, but they tend to see everything they do as a valuable investment of their time. This might involve charging no fee or reduced fees for speaking engagements, talks or lectures as a strategy to help build their profile and expand their networks; offering free samples or trial products/services to raise brand awareness; or making their expertise available to a group or company in exchange for something of equal or greater benefit.

Understandably, not everyone is in a position to raise their profile or business by doing free talks, workshops or any other self-promotional activity that brings in zero revenue. However, it is possible to seek out activities that will help you to communicate what you do more effectively and also set you apart from your competition.

4. In Robin S. Sharma's *The Monk Who Sold His Ferrari*, the value of time is highlighted when a character in the book, Julian Mantle, declares, 'Don't let others steal your time. Be wary of time thieves … people will respect you more when they see that you are a person who values [his] time. They will realize that your time is precious and they will value it.' R. S. Sharma, *The Monk Who Sold His Ferrari* (London: HarperElement, 2004), p. 166.

Remember

Throughout your career, some sacrifices are inevitable and become the trade-off to achieving your goals. But this requires finding a suitable balance between business and personal life. It is crucial to regard this time as a valuable commodity. It is important to remember how your perception of time can change as you enter new landscapes, so ensure that you value your time and your expertise and, equally, that others value and respect your time.

Be **Seen**

Consider how freeing up some of your working hours could increase the time you could devote to your own project and further impact on your networks.

Be **Heard**

Make sure that you are recognised for valuing and taking your time seriously. Augment the importance of value in every idea or project and let this become part of your voice.

Get **Noticed**

Activities such as self-marketing or product/service development is a good investment of your time and will contribute to raising your profile and getting you noticed.

PART 2
ReAct

In the next seven chapters, we will
explore some proven methods and
techniques, as well as some innovative
approaches, that will enable you
to apply new ways of thinking to
building distinctiveness in the way you
communicate your personal, career,
business and entrepreneurial prospects.

Let's go!

14
Face to Face with Challenge

At various points in your professional and personal life, you will inevitably encounter new challenges that take you out of your zone of familiarity and test your resilience. When you face a challenge head on you will inevitably make choices that test your commitment, durability and perseverance, as well as the strength of your support network. However, it is crucial to remain open to fresh challenges and to recognise them as an opportunity to push yourself in areas that may lead to new knowledge and experience.

Two rooms, one reality

Picture the scenario. You are on a journey to the 'land of your ambitions' – the place where your ideas, desires, aspirations and goals can be realised. However, in order to get there, you have to pass through one of two rooms.

Room A is a brightly lit space. It will provide you with a clear road map and the support you need to get you to your destination. It is the safe option. There are some rules and conditions, but as long as you stick to them you will soon be in possession of a golden passport to enter the land of your ambitions.

Room B is a darker and more hazy space. Here things are less certain and less predictable. You may encounter other individuals, but none of them will have the key that will get you to the land of your ambitions, although they might point you in the right direction. Without a map you face an unknown journey. There are rules here too but also freedom to break them. There is no 100% guarantee that you will ever reach the land of your ambitions in Room B, but you might if you persevere.

While Room A offers certainty, Room B offers more scope to realise your ideas and dreams. Which would you choose – Room A or Room B?

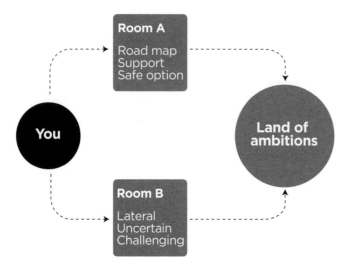

Depending on who you are and where you are in your career, you will either be seeking guarantees and a safe bet or chance and the unpredictable. We all need some level of certainty in our lives, but some of us are more open to serendipity.

In the reality of business and professional life, it is questionable whether Room A – the safety net of a dependable future landscape – actually exists. What most of us need is the courage and ambition to inhabit Room B. Many entrepreneurs and individuals developing new ideas embrace and welcome being in that zone of not knowing exactly how or when their idea will generate interest and create opportunities, but a combination of commitment, drive and enthusiasm all contribute to helping them to view the challenge positively.

Burn up the back burner

It is incredible how many of us often wait to initiate a project until the time is absolutely right, whether it's a career move or a new business venture. Usually, we are waiting for that magical moment when time stops and we can jump on board and take action. But the longer we wait, and the longer we stare at the abyss, the larger it gets. Procrastination feeds the void and fosters doubt, anxiety, fear and yet more reasons to justify why it is still not the right time to get started.

One way to overcome procrastination is to resist the temptation to begin things at the start of next week, next month or, even worse, next year. I am sure you have given yourself start dates for embarking on a project, such as revisiting your profile or making contact with a key person, and inevitably (like some diet plans) it is destined to start on a Monday, right? This can be a recipe for failure as, undoubtedly, factors creep in that postpone your progress. As this happens, your relationship with time changes, and the 'back burner' wins the day, month or year.

Instead, adopt a more holistic approach to negotiating project timescales and deadlines. We all know that tasks are not defined by hours, days or calendar markers. Aim to operate within these more flexible time frames, and avoid the starting block of a specific date or time.

Entering unknown territory

As you navigate your way through your career, you are bound to encounter new areas that not only challenge you, but which have the potential to disrupt the perceptions of those around you. As a relative newcomer to an environment, you will bring with you the aura of something new, something alien to the inhabitants of that landscape. At best, it is embraced as a welcome breath of fresh air, innovative and game changing. At worst, you may be deemed as a threat.

This is to be expected. The challenge is not necessarily to fit in, but to get others to fit into *your* worldview and system of beliefs. Standing by what is true to you or your brand requires an immense level of self-belief, courage and downright determination. We often see this when individuals or brands diversify into areas far removed from their original field of expertise. The brand proliferation of Virgin, from record label to air travel and multimedia empire, is an inspiring example for anyone facing the challenge of venturing into a new area of business.

One creative who has faced many challenges when entering relatively unfamiliar territory is world-renowned fashion designer Ozwald Boateng. Boateng stands out as one of the few designers who *is* his brand – he looks like a catwalk model from one of his own shows. As well as being a leading figure for his brand, he is also his own best advert.

When he created his brand at the tender age of 18, one of Boateng's biggest challenges was entering the fashion industry where the established order had held sway for centuries. British born and of Ghanaian origin, Boateng conquered new territory as the youngest and first black man to have an outlet in London's prestigious Savile Row. But he also endeavoured to push the boundaries of the Establishment by merging the realms of tailoring and fashion. On the challenge of shaking up the industry he said:

" *When I started ... department stores were either very fashion, or very tailored, so the two never mixed. I mixed it, and they said you're too tailored for fashion and too fashion for tailoring. So I had to move the market. So that's what I did. So I was very unique. And then everyone looked, and said, do you know what, that makes sense, it really makes sense.*[1]

It wasn't long before his distinctive fusion of traditional tailoring and bold colours became his signature trademark. His broad and courageous outlook on changing the perceptions of industry, heritage and culture has been one of Boateng's hallmarks, and it is a legacy that continues today as the brand infiltrates new and emerging markets.

1. D. Aitkenhead, 'Ozwald Boateng: Does My Head Look Big In This?', *The Guardian* (9 March 2012). Available at: http://www.theguardian.com/fashion/2012/mar/09/ozwald-boateng-fashion-designer-tailor.

Reframing the unknown – a different perspective

It can be helpful to establish a fresh perspective on a problem by reframing it. If you are too close to it, whether it's developing your profile, finding a new job, seeking a promotion or developing a business that stands out among the crowd, it can be hard to see a way out. Reframing helps in a number of ways:

- Objectivity, or simply standing back from the problem, requires you to assess what resources, skills and support are needed. It also allows you to look at the challenge from a fresh angle.

- Asking better questions can create new opportunities and reveal novel approaches and solutions.

- By asking a few key questions you can often turn a problem into an opportunity, leading to new insights and expanding the range of potential outcomes.

- Adjust the phrasing of the challenge from, 'How will this be achieved?', to a more definitive, 'This can be achieved – what resources do I need?'

Too often, we are too focused on finding the big solution. But sometimes new insights only emerge when we find a new way of looking at a problem by rephrasing the question or reframing the challenge.

A challenge beyond photo sharing

A new venture, product or service launching in an environment where more established or larger operators or individuals already exist will certainly face the pressures of building and maintaining a presence. Co-founders Kevin Systrom and Mike Krieger's Instagram more than caught the attention of Facebook – it was subsequently acquired for a reported US$1 billion.

The challenge Instagram surmounted went much deeper than just better provision of photo sharing. If the objective was simply to develop the best platform, then arguably that was not enough make an impact or get noticed. The challenge was repackaged as a way to improve or enhance the customer experience – how to create a product that changed people's lives. This, by default, opened up greater opportunities for standing out among their rivals. Systrom claims that Instagram was never about photo sharing; he said it was more about 'communicating a moment (to someone). It just happens to be an image.'[2] With the increasing demand for mobile technology, it was clear that Instagram's future resided within the arena of apps, smartphones and tablets – there was no need to take on traditional web-based models such as Flickr.[3]

In my own experience in business and academic practice, whenever I have faced an insurmountable challenge, a natural defence mechanism kicks in. The pragmatic and protective part of me steps in to ensure that I don't get my fingers burned – the internal gremlin who is more than happy to reside in the cosy comfort of the status quo. However, this is quickly overcome by an even stronger element that fights back and urges me to move forward.

ReAct

Here are four of the mindsets that you can adopt to reinforce your position when facing the unknown:

- **Adopt a 'no turning back' frame of mind** – imagine preparing for a race, but knowing you could simply quit or turn back if you wished. What would be the point? You need a determination to commit with no room for capitulation.

2. See D. Terdiman, 'Instagram's Systrom: We're "Not a Photography Company"', *CNET* (31 May 2013). Available at: http://www.cnet.com/uk/news/instagrams-systrom-were-not-a-photography-company/.

3. In an interview for *The Guardian*, Systrom stated, 'It wasn't a choice … Instagram just would not work on the web if we'd asked people to sign up for a service where they can upload a photo of what they did five hours ago. Instagram is special because it's in the moment and the photo you're seeing from your friends is live'. J. Kiss, 'Kevin Systrom, Instagram's Man of Vision, Now Eyes Up World Domination', *The Guardian* (11 October 2013). Available at: http://www.theguardian.com/technology/2013/oct/11/instagram-kevin-systrom-world-domination.

- **Analyse what you have to lose** – in doing so, you are outlining some of the key factors that are important to you. The spirit we encounter from young and vibrant individuals is often inspiring. Unfortunately, as we get older, the stakes are higher – rent, mortgages, bills and other liabilities. However, if you are able to assess the risks strategically, you are more likely to make better informed decisions.

- **Gain a new perspective** – looking sideways at a challenge often yields fresh viewpoints. Ask more questions rather than chasing your tail by asking the same questions. Rephrasing a question is a sure-fire way to create new insights.

- **Prepare to hit the wall of doubt** – you will inevitably arrive at the point at which doubt stares you in the face. You will be self-critical, you will question yourself and your motives. However, make sure that this re-examination is constructive and you do not lose sight of your objectives.

A combination of reframing and rephrasing questions and seeking new perspectives is certain to adjust your relationship with new and exciting challenges. And remember: effective personal and professional development needs to be fed by regular challenges that test you and your practices.

ReAct

| 1 Adopt a 'no turning back' frame of mind | 2 Analyse what you have to lose | 3 Gain a new perspective | 4 Prepare to hit the wall of doubt |

15
Satellite Harmony

How do you communicate your idea, service, product or professional profile to the needs of a national or global audience? The digital age has brought with it more demanding consumers who can access a host of media, news, events, presentations and data whenever they want. Elements such as your expertise, qualities, experience, professional profile and knowledge – your satellites – are no longer localised and confined to the 9 to 5.

So, how can your product transcend time zones, borders and cultures? How do the elements you have created communicate to a global audience? And, more importantly, are the elements you put out in harmony with each other, with a coherent and consistent message?

Launch the elements into orbit

I was once involved in a meeting to discuss a creative project with a potential client. I was told that the client's web developer, who was going to look after the online and social media part of the assignment, would be joining us. When he arrived, he presented his thoughts and opinions on the project, as well as providing some valuable insights and perspectives based on his previous experience of running major web and social media projects. He described numerous projects, some more successful than others, and was candid about why some were more successful than others.

Our meeting was drawing to a close and the web developer was preparing to leave slightly earlier. Before he left, he scribbled some web addresses and other online links on a note pad and left them with us. The meeting continued for a short while, but we found ourselves still paraphrasing the web developer, as well as pointing and gesturing to his now vacant chair, as if he were an invisible man! As the discussion progressed, we still made reference to many of the key points he had raised, not just about social media but also referring back to his own experiences in previous projects.

It was not necessarily the web developer's knowledge of social media that became our reference point. Instead, it was more the amalgam of events, circumstances and experiences that shaped his story that was so fascinating and which was part of his lasting impression. More importantly, there were numerous factors that continued to communicate for him and represent him in his absence. He had, metaphorically speaking, 'satellites'. These satellites included a combination of tangible and intangible elements – knowledge, appearance, persona, URLs, blogs, experiences and story. All these functioned in harmony to build a coherent picture and to function as a holistic entity that, in many ways, contributed to his personal 'brand'.

So, how can you ensure that you have a range of satellites that function effectively as part of your personal brand?

Being plural and creating harmony

Having satellites at work and operating in tandem creates opportunities to stop dividing your time and attention and instead enter a far more productive and dynamic realm of plurality.

We all have a range of elements that can perform the role of satellite for us; ideally, all our satellites are working constantly and remotely in synergy – or 'satellite harmony'. Satellites can include *tangibles*, such as products, services, online profiles, websites, articles, blogs, films and brand identities, and *intangibles*, such as persona, tone of communication, ethos, principles and reputation. Regardless of the medium, how do your satellites function to serve your objectives?

In much the same way that we might consider residual income as regular remuneration that continues to pay out after a job has been completed, we can also look at the relative notion of 'residual connectivity'. In other words, staying on the radar of the people in your network on a regular basis via a range of satellites that are in harmony,

Satellite Harmony

● tangibles   ○ intangibles

consistent in their message and continuously communicating who you are or what you do to make people want to do business with you.

As these satellites are open all hours they need careful maintenance and nurturing: you cannot leave them unsupervised for long periods of time. It is the strategic management of tangible and intangible elements that will ensure you are relevant and current, uppermost in the minds of your network and community. In turn, this will ensure that you are constantly being remembered, considered, recommended and nominated.

Alignment and synchronicity

In order to ensure satellite harmony, you need to make clear distinctions between tangible and intangible satellites. Tangible satellites (e.g. websites, blogs, promotional material, merchandise) are visible and immediate to your audience. These are very much within your control. As purveyors of your brand or profile, it is important that key messages and objectives are aligned and consistent.

Any intangibles embedded in your message should be also coherent across your tangible satellites. For example, your ethos, knowledge and principles are what make you credible, so these should be present in the tangibles to seamlessly convey your message, ideals and objectives.

Managing satellite perceptions

While your satellites can successfully work for you to communicate who you are and what you do, it is not always as easy to get an authentic understanding of people's perceptions, especially if there are inconsistencies or disparities in your satellites. It is down to you alone to detect if your satellites are failing to communicate the message and tone you intend.

How do you do this? You can get some idea of the strength of your reputation by requesting feedback or by regularly assessing and reviewing your profile, business or ideas. However, how you think you come across and how the outside world actually views you may be very different, so it is important to be detached and objective when analysing your own practice.

This is challenging enough in itself, but let's explore one of the intangible satellites mentioned above – ethos. Ethos includes character, essence, atmosphere, mood, feeling, spirit and morals. These are all affirmative, brand defining qualities, but how do you know whether what you are putting out actually works? One approach would be to get an objective viewpoint from those who have interacted with you professionally. Often, people will simply use some of these terms in profiles or brand statements from their own perspective. However, your qualities can only really be authenticated by those who have experience of your expertise. For example, word of mouth, one of the most primitive forms of marketing, really is in the hands of your audience and network.

Avoid the wrath of *Viva Voce* scorned

Although 'word of mouth' is a much overused phrase, it is critical to a flourishing business. Unfortunately, it is almost impossible to see it in action – until, that is, it is translated into real actions or firm connections. However, you should aim to ensure that word of mouth is always working positively for you.

It might be useful to personify the rather abstract notion of word of mouth to gain a new perspective. Let us call her *Viva Voce*[1] (indulge me for a moment!).

" Viva Voce *understands you. She knows who you are, what you do. She knows your entire academic and professional backstory.* Viva Voce *is self-sufficient to a degree and can work automatically, but she needs constant fuelling and re-energising via your tangible and intangible satellites. Without this she cannot function. Once equipped, she has all the resources she needs to ensure the careful management of your profile, skills, values, practices and achievements. She works twenty-four hours a day, seven days a week and asks for nothing in return. She is loyal. She is there to safeguard your reputation, so she also keeps the negative tentacles of rumour at bay.*

1. The Latin phrase, *viva voce*, literally translated means 'with living voice', but it is also associated with the idiom 'word of mouth'.

You need to ensure that the satellites you generate are authentic and true to you. Viva Voce is astute and knows immediately if anything you communicate is not aligned with your true self. She also knows that you would discredit yourself if you tried to fake values or attributes.

You need to live up to her good work. If you are unable to deliver on the good standing she has built for you, she can do no more as the ugly face of bad reputation, unreliability and deceit rear their heads, fuelled by the headwinds of social networks and other news mediums. She knows as well as you that it would take an age to fix or reverse any negative perceptions about you. But she is at work to ensure this never happens.

In short, you need to genuinely identify with the qualities you communicate so as to give others a genuine reason why you should stick in their minds or why they should seek out your expertise.[2] In a digital age where blogs and social media form part of the landscape, it is important for your satellites to work in harmony across various physical and non-physical spaces, digital and non-digital, human and technological. Give people a good reason to talk about you.[3]

2. There are dozens of books on word of mouth marketing, but I think one of the more memorable ones is *Word of Mouth Marketing* by Andy Sernovitz, who comments: 'Earn the respect and recommendation of your customers, and they will do the rest. Treat people well, and they will do your marketing for you, for free. Be interesting or be invisible ... You just have to give people something to talk about.' A. Sernovitz, *Word of Mouth Marketing: How Smart Companies Get People Talking* (Austin, TX: Greenleaf Book Group, 2012), p. xvi–xvii.

3. A book that explores reputation is Rob Brown's *How to Build Your Reputation*. He observes: 'Sometimes it's not how good you are that counts, so much as how good others say you are.' R. Brown, *How to Build Your Reputation: The Secrets of Becoming the 'Go To' Professional in a Crowded Marketplace* (Penryn: Ecademy Press, 2007), p. 18.

4. N. Nahai, *Webs of Influence: The Psychology of Online Persuasion* (Harlow: Pearson Education, 2012).

Interview with Nathalie Nahai

Nathalie Nahai is the Web Psychologist, an award-winning speaker and bestselling author of *Webs of Influence: The Psychology of Online Persuasion*.[4] She engages in the complex management of her brand with offline activity, such as talks, lectures, events and conferences, and online platforms, including a blog, articles, videos, website (www.thewebpsychologist.com), podcasts and e-training. I interviewed Nathalie and asked her about the key elements and commonalities of the Web Psychologist brand that are consistent throughout her online and offline activities.

When it comes to developing your ideas or brand, one of the most important factors for success, whichever channel you're using, is your ability to be yourself. When I originally set out to build up my brand across social media, in bookstores and onstage, I was working on the assumption that to attract followers and establish a good reputation, I would need to present a very professional front across all media. But when communicating online via social media, blogs and Twitter, I was able to explore new ground and start playing with personas in more expressive ways that reflected my personality, while still being able to communicate and drive the main principles of my brand.

Whether you are writing a blog, uploading videos or giving a keynote, the people you are connecting with are not there just because they want your knowledge – they're there because you are the one who is imparting it. So, it is vital that you can express your individuality throughout all mediums with authenticity.

Finally, it is advisable to tailor your communication to best fit the channel through which you are disseminating it, while ensuring there is consistency in the tone and delivery throughout. As you develop tangible or intangible elements, your core values should be the common thread that runs through everything you do, so that every output you create is suffused with your personal brand and your own distinctive DNA.

Navigating the satellites

- **Know what you can see but can't touch** – get an understanding of the elements of your brand or profile that are tangible and intangible. The tangibles in the physical realm are easier to replicate and they are also very effective vehicles for communicating the intangibles. The intangibles are how others define you.

- **Show up and show off** – it is pointless having an array of satellites that all work in harmony if you are not showing them off; even more so with the tangible satellites. You need to be constantly pushing these elements into the consciousness of your audience.

- **Match the tones** – where possible, try to find out what people are saying when they refer you, and ensure that this is aligned with or incorporated into your tangibles. Revisit your intangibles to ascertain if they are a true reflection of your brand.

- **Constantly evaluate** – you need to check regularly (perhaps with a devil's advocate – see Chapter 6) that your satellites are functioning and communicating who you are. More to the point, are they distinctive?

- **Stay calm and focused** – it's not all about being online. While blogs and social media have contributed to the democratisation of publishing and the sharing of ideas, the majority of our interactions still take place face to face. Blogs, online communities and comments have made it easier to get feedback and gauge audience reactions, and this can start to help you develop a better understanding of what conversations are taking place, but the real skill is being able to process or act on feedback, whether it is online or word of mouth.

- **Transmit your passion** – your passion and drive help to communicate your values. It is important that others are able to sense your commitment, drive, purpose and enthusiasm.

ReAct

1
Know what you can see but can't touch

2
Show up and show off

3
Match the tones

4
Constantly evaluate

5
Stay calm and focused

6
Transmit your passion

16
Spot the Difference

No matter what stage you at are in your career, you need to broadcast your individuality and adopt methods that best project your distinctiveness. Consequently, if you are communicating using a similar message, tone, voice, vocabulary or technique as your competitors, your audience will be challenged to identify your individuality.

Essentially, we all have something different to offer through the amalgam of the varied experiences that have helped to shape us and our ideas. A curious mindset and an inquisitive attitude will equip you to question (not necessarily resist) traditions and conventions; to identify obstacles that stand between you, your objectives and making a difference; to create firmer ground from which to build distinctiveness; and to develop confidence in what you are, why you do it and how you are different.

In this chapter, we will explore some of the key factors that can change and heighten your awareness of how you communicate your core attributes to others, but also how others perceive you, your ideas, brand, product or service.

Message within the bottle

Stop for a moment and look around you. You will, no doubt, be able to see an array of products, services, messages, suggestions, advertising slogans, brands and so on that all started their existence as an idea. They are the manifestation of a once grand vision that had to be made distinctive from competing ideas in order to be implemented.

In many cases, the tacit elements of an idea or brand are invisible to the naked eye, which makes the importance of transmitting those characteristic factors even more essential. The design, brand or meaning behind these ideas, services or products represents a complex application of brand vision, strategy and development. They have been carefully designed to engage with our senses and curiosity.[1]

1. Alina Wheeler delivers a very comprehensive guide for managers and designers: 'Branding is about seizing every opportunity to express why people should choose one brand over another ... A strong brand stands out in a densely crowded marketplace ... How a brand is perceived affects its success, regardless of whether it's a start-up, a non-profit, or a product.' A. Wheeler, *Designing Brand Identity: An Essential Guide for the Whole Branding Team* (4th edn) (Hoboken, NJ: John Wiley & Sons, 2002), p. 2.

Understanding how and why people make the decision to choose you, your company, product or service should form the basis of your differentiation, thereby enabling you to stand out in saturated markets. Knowing what makes you special will help you to win the attention of people who, for now, know very little or nothing about you.

When considering differentiation, think about the following questions:

• How can you ensure that you create an impact that instils trust in the people you want to do business with and at the same time convey distinctiveness that puts you ahead of your competitors?

• Are you confident that the techniques and strategies you are deploying are not being used by your rivals?

• How are you really any different from other companies, brands or products that are demanding the attention of this audience?

When you can start to clearly identify and articulate what makes you different, you will be able to communicate who you are and what you do simply and effectively.

Different is better than better

If you know or have ever met identical twins, it is fascinating how similar they can be – not just their visual appearance but their expressions, mannerisms and tone. They may even adopt the same fashion sense and have more or less the same body shape and build. It is often not until you engage in conversation, or interact on a deeper level, that a host of differences emerge. You soon discover how different they are – from their interests, likes and dislikes to career goals, motivations and many more factors. We always need to look beyond the aesthetic.

Now consider your own brand, business or venture: to the outside world might you be almost identical to your competitors? This could surface in the language, tone, messages or behaviours that you adopt. Make sure that you understand the underlying defining characteristics that truly set you apart from others, beyond the superficialities, by amplifying what makes you different. I have outlined below some approaches that explore how your personal story and defining factors can help people to see beyond the superficial. This is the distinction between being different and being better. While naturally we want to be better than our rivals, in fact it is individuality that is the key defining factor. With less emphasis on being better, and more focus on distinctiveness, you can set yourself apart from your rivals.[2]

Once upon a time ...

Story can be utilised as a powerful tool to convey experiences, vision, meaning and authenticity that signal your individuality. This type of narrative is not to do with tall tales; it is more about the collection of original experiences and events that have shaped your backstory.

Your story is the result of a discrete set of experiences, events, beliefs and feelings. Playing on this can assist you to stand out and avoid the perils of common rhetoric. Elements of story can also help you to resonate with your audiences and target groups, and can have a significant impact on how people connect with you.[3]

Two apples, one man and an audience

It is easy to fall into the trap of using common themes and language when describing ourselves or our product. It is good practice to be alert to this problem and apply methods to ensure that you are continually differentiating. So, how can you start to develop a mindset that lifts you above and beyond people, products or businesses that, on paper, appear to be relatively similar?

2. Jules Goddard and Tony Eccles observe: 'Aiming merely to be better than competitors is perilous. While not guaranteeing failure, it has the perverse effect of making competitors more alike, if only because each of them will tend to define "betterness" in identical terms. So the more competitors pursue "betterness", the more they will converge upon the same solutions.' J. Goddard and T. Eccles, *Uncommon Sense, Common Nonsense: Why Some Organisations Consistently Outperform Others* (London: Profile Books, 2013), p. 4.

3. In *Make your Idea Matter*, Bernadette Jiwa describes using 'story' to make connection: 'When customer and investors (or maybe even you) don't understand your story ... your brand fails to connect ... When people really "get it" your brand has the potential to attract investors, dominate a niche and reinvent a market.' B. Jiwa, *Make Your Idea Matter: Stand Out with a Better Story* (N.p.: Story of Telling Press, 2012), p. 32.

During one of my recent workshops, I took the audience through an exercise to demonstrate how to transcend the boundaries of predictable behaviour, terms and rhetoric in order to differentiate themselves in crowded markets. Equipped with just two apples and a curious eyebrow raised audience, I took them through three main stages:

1. I divided them into two groups. After handing an apple to each group, we agreed that apart from a few minor blemishes they were two rather identical apples. I asked each group to observe their apple and in three minutes to write down and describe the fruit using just five words. As expected, each group returned words like 'round', 'fruit', 'green', 'crunchy' and 'healthy'. They had fulfilled the first part of the exercise by describing what they saw directly.

2. Next, I asked them to describe the apples but to omit the words they had used in the first stage. As this was a slightly more challenging task, I doubled the time and the number of words they could use. With more time and more words they were destined to be more descriptive about the apple, right? Actually, both groups struggled to define the apple without using any of the words from stage 1 and resorted to non-descriptors such as 'nice', 'fruit salad' and 'apple crumble'. I suspected that this stage would probably be the most challenging for the groups.

3. Finally, I asked them to describe the fruit again, again omitting any words from the two previous stages. This time they had to really sell the apple to me, perhaps attaching a story or meaning. There were no limitations on the number of words and no restrictions as to how they could communicate it. They were given the same amount of time as for stage 2, but the outcomes couldn't have been more different.

This task opened up the creative output of each group – they now started to think in full colour as opposed to the narrow confines of the previous stages. One group explored the source of the apple as one of the main elements of their story. They were able to communicate this more effectively, but also with more excitement, zest and humour. The two groups' definitions of the apples were very different, but it was their approach to exploring different narratives that made them distinctive – for example, one group focused on culture and geography as part of their narrative.

This wasn't an exercise in simply making up a story to fit the object. On the contrary, it demonstrated the potential of story to explore how best to communicate the apple's singularity through factors beneath the surface. This process is outlined in the diagram below.

Before
similiar skills, qualifications, descriptors, qualities, common terms

Process

re-identify

Over the three stages, the process of moving away from common terms and descriptors challenges individuals to consider elements of narrative, story, experiences or meaning

re-define

After
similar skills, qualifications, qualities remain the same but the process of highlighting story, narrative and experiences has altered

Exhibits x and y are used to symbolise relatively similar or identical entities. This process demonstrates the significance of transcending the boundaries of predictable behaviour, common terms and rhetoric in order to differentiate effectively

Following the exercise, I explained to the groups that although this might have appeared trivial, my intention was to highlight the errors that many people make when describing or promoting themselves (stage 1). Stage 3 illustrated the significance of going beyond the predictable. Also, by omitting the standard rhetoric that might be used by competitors, they were more likely to think in descriptive and original ways.

Going further – the 3D factor

While it is important to establish story as a key element when differentiating yourself or your business, is story alone enough?

Firstly, it is essential that your narrative is not shoehorned in for the sake of it; it should be authentic and convey meaningful experiences. Secondly, you need to use a multidimensional approach to understanding what sets you apart – what I call 'the 3D factor'. The 3D factor requires you to identify three distinguishing aspects about yourself or your product. These should be broad categories – for example, culture, product or location – that can be drilled down into and defined in more detail.

These defining factors do not work alone: in isolation they are not enough to distinguish you from your rivals (e.g. you could not claim that what makes you distinctive is your amazing personality, your products and the area you operate within). It is the cross-pollination and interplay of these factors, as well as your deeper analysis, that will start to build a very different picture.

The diagram opposite uses the example of culture, product and location. The first stage is to describe in more detail what is distinctive about each factor. The next stage is to ensure that there is cohesion between these factors – that is, they all relate to you (or your brand) rather than simply being plucked out of the air. The amalgam of these more detailed outcomes is what becomes *your* definitive story and, therefore, what makes you distinct.

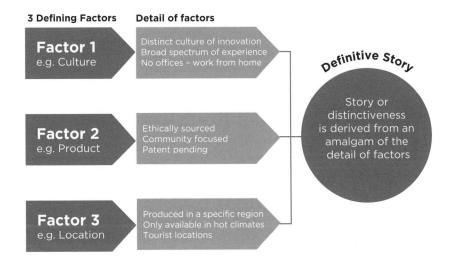

3 Defining Factors

Detail of factors

Factor 1
e.g. Culture

Distinct culture of innovation
Broad spectrum of experience
No offices – work from home

Factor 2
e.g. Product

Ethically sourced
Community focused
Patent pending

Factor 3
e.g. Location

Produced in a specific region
Only available in hot climates
Tourist locations

Definitive Story

Story or distinctiveness is derived from an amalgam of the detail of factors

The age of the specialists

There is an increasing trend for individuals and companies to specialise and find niches within which to operate. Specialisms are often perceived as a way to find a more focused remit and segregate from the mass of competitors.[4] A strong brand vision, purpose and, of course, customer loyalty are essential to ensure that your niche market remains relatively undisrupted by competitors that could impact on your market share.

4. Rob Brown briefly touches on the notion of 'niche proliferation': 'the age of the specialist is here ... the age of the generalist has gone. You must consider niching to survive.' R. Brown, *How to Build Your Reputation: The Secrets of Becoming the 'Go To' Professional in a Crowded Marketplace* (Penryn: Ecademy Press, 2007), p. 41.

Interview with Martin Roach

One company which has differentiated to reach a more targeted audience is branding and communications agency Brands With Values. They believe that values are at the heart of communities and communities are at the heart of brands. I interviewed their director of innovation, Martin Roach, about how this has helped them to differentiate in their field.

RM: How does putting values at the heart of your business help you to differentiate from your competitors?

MR: When I first set up our company we were an ethical branding agency and that defined who we worked with. Ultimately that was quite limiting. If you try to define yourselves purely by a small number of clients then you miss out on quite a large picture, quite a large amount of work. And so we found it limiting if we said we were working with charities, not-for-profits and universities. That doesn't necessarily make you ethical; that just means that you're not answering a whole group of questions that you need to answer.

The notion of a value-led business was a way to try to answer those difficult questions. It was about realising that we're all human and we all have very similar interests. So, it was really based on my own values and trying to ask those questions. And the more I was able to be in tune with myself and what I thought about, the more informed I was and the more confident I was to go out into the marketplace with the ideology of values at the heart of our business.

RM: How do you communicate this point of differentiation to an audience who might have a more conventional association with graphic design, branding and communications?

MR: I think the biggest challenge for us and other design agencies is to try to show how you can add value to a business through design. So many elements of design are a lot more automated, specifically web design, and obviously that's a big part of the marketing mix. There are also agencies that don't have the same boundaries they used to have in the past. So it's quite conceivable that a PR agency, a design agency, a branding agency or a web agency could deliver a brand for you. So how, as a client, do you know which of these you should go with? We've focused on how your values can be shown through all of your touch points, through all the things that you actually do. And then we get involved in those touch points as a result. So it's a very different process, a very different communicative process with the client.

RM: What would you consider to be some of the most important things that any new emerging company or individual needs to be aware of to stand out in a competitive industry, business or professional environment?

MR: I think any emerging (or established) companies or individuals with ideas need to ask themselves what their true purpose is and what makes them different. There are lots of other organisations that are arguably doing the same thing or similar. There's got to be a compelling reason to create something new. Once you can start to answer that, then I think you can begin to build on it. It is important not to lose sight of your original focus and purpose. It's very easy to do. You get caught up and you think, 'Oh well, this is a new trend. I'm just going to follow that.' But if it moves you away from that original purpose that you were set up for, the further away from that you move, the more difficult you'll find it. You just begin to blend in.

Also, being recognised as a trusted advisor is core to anyone's brand; whether you are an accountant, solicitor or in the creative industries, it helps to differentiate from competitors. The key is to aim to be an authority in the field where clients and colleagues respect your knowledge and experience.

Avoiding the photo finish

- **You x 2: your move** – you are positioned next to an individual almost identical to you in skills, experience and aptitude, and are head to head to win a project. You are well matched and with almost nothing to separate you. Consider what distinctive qualities you can call on that will win you the job.

- **Make the difference** – consider going through a similar exercise as depicted in the two apples task. Describe what you do using just five key words. Then describe yourself without those words. Finally, describe yourself in a memorable way so that people will remember you.

- **Go boldly down unbeaten paths** – finding a niche area and aiming to specialise in that area will help you to define what you do more easily. It will also help you to target your audience more effectively.

- **Revisit the Great Anti-Glossary** (Chapter 7) – ensure that the terms you use to describe yourself do not fall into the realm of common rhetoric. While many of the positive epithets you use to describe what you do may be true, consider your audience and the possibility that they have heard it all before. Invest time in exploring more meaningful, authentic terms that speak for you alone.

ReAct

1	**2**	**3**	**4**
You x 2: your move	**Make the difference**	**Go boldly down unbeaten paths**	**Revisit the Great Anti-Glossary**

17
Averting Skill Disruption

What is your profession or industry going to look like in the near future or in, say, five or ten years' time? What factors might have an impact on the growth or stability of your sector? If you plan to or currently work as a solicitor or a baker (random, I know), we can pretty much safely bet that those industries will experience less dramatic change and impact than the music industry or publishing.[1] Still, no one can be certain of the changes that will affect the economic or commercial landscape – we can only speculate.

So, how can you be sure that you have the necessary skills, values and attributes that you will need now and in the future, whether you work in same sector or decide on a total career change? With many industries facing ongoing disruption, you need to safeguard the relevance of your skills and values by undertaking continuing professional development and training. More importantly, you need to ensure that your skills and values are transferrable in case your industry heads for extinction.[2]

You only have to visit your local supermarket to see how technological advancements have had a profound impact on the food retail sector. Self-service tills have reduced the number of personnel that used to carry out this traditional role; the task has been literally handed over to the consumer, turning us all into check-out boys and girls. Computerisation, the immediacy of the web and the expansion of choice have all given more control to the consumer, but they have also impacted on employment trends, making various skills and occupations redundant.[3]

So, how can you ensure that you don't become another statistic in the technology body count? The answer lies in building skills and qualities that are outside the remit of computerisation and automation. This requires exploring fields and qualities that are the 'antithesis of computerisation',[4] employing creativity, originality, thinking, expression, craftsmanship, deliberation and sometimes, quite simply, the human touch. From laying bricks to the creation of a novel or screenplay, there

1. Simon Waldman observes how digital has had a profound impact on businesses and industry in his book, *Creative Disruption*.

2. Gwen Parkes cites statistics and research conducted by the US Bureau of Labor Statistics and observes that various industries, such as department stores and newspaper publishing, will inevitably become obsolete and disappear off the economic horizon: 'Unfortunately, many people working in these industries are finding that jobs no longer exist as it is hard to keep pace with the advancing economy and technologies that society demands.' G. Parks, 'Jobs That No Longer Exist: 10 Industries Heading for Extinction', *AoI Jobs* (17 December 2009). Available at: http://jobs.aol.com/articles/2009/12/17/10-industries-heading-for-extinction/.

3. Carl Benedikt Frey and Michael A. Osborne estimate that 47% of employment in the United States is at risk from the advancement of computerisation and automation. See C. B. Frey and M. A. Osborne, 'The Future of Employment: How Susceptible Are Jobs to Computerisation?' (17 September 2013). Available at: http://www.oxfordmartin.ox.ac.uk/downloads/academic/The_Future_of_Employment.pdf.

are some things that cannot be delivered by complex algorithms and source codes.

It is also vital to cultivate qualities that cannot be replicated or outsourced, qualities that require us to be expressive, mindful or convey emotion. For example, being able to reflect, impart knowledge or share experiences through narratives and stories can be aided by computerised processes but never replaced. It requires strategies and approaches that make us, as humans, indispensable.[5] While software systems have enabled all sorts of people to develop their own websites, for example, the human mind is still very much the driver of content, emotion and vision.

Broadening the scope of skills

Both hard skills (i.e. teachable, quantifiable), such as proficiency with software and language expertise, and soft skills (i.e. people skills), such as relationships, interactions, communication and dialogue, are essential in the context of career and professional development. Later in this chapter we will explore how you can re-communicate these skills, applying them to a broader and more diverse range of sectors, and also with the view to creating a distinctive brand.

Financial crises have had profound economic consequences for many industries around the world, as well as the communities they serve. When a major car manufacturing plant or factory, for example, closes down an entire city can collapse from unemployment – just look at Detroit. These circumstances do not just impact on an industry in the abstract. Individuals' skills can also be interrupted when faced with demotion, redundancy or relocation. I call this 'skill disruption'.

Skill disruption can happen in almost any industry, especially if workers have been trained and/or employed solely in that sector for most of their working life. Clearly, being saddled with skills that have been

4. Amol Rajan argues that there are creative limitations to 'robots' and that certain fields may never be totally disrupted by digital or technological advancement: 'Machines can't do creativity. They'll never produce great works of art, write memorable stanzas, design exquisite museums or compose beautiful symphonies.' A. Rajan, 'Be Creative If You Want to Outsmart the Robots', *London Evening Standard* (13 February 2013). Available at: http://www.standard.co.uk/comment/amol-rajan-be-creative-if-you-want-to-outsmart-the-robots-9125649.html.

5. Seth Godin says: 'You don't become indispensable merely because you are different. But the only way to be indispensable is to be different' (Godin, *Linchpin*, p. 27).

displaced or become obsolete can have major consequences for future employability. It is also a concern for individuals who have trained or gained qualifications in a particular sector, only to discover that it is an oversaturated market where the number of applicants far outweighs the number of work opportunities.

So, make sure that you are applying your skills wisely to a broad range of sectors and settings.

Early focus – saint or sinner?

We are encouraged to make career defining decisions at a very early stage in our lives, usually at school or during further/higher education. These important decisions have a profound impact on the early part of our career and the interactions, networks and environments in which we operate. Granted, focus is valuable and can help to direct our abilities and talents towards making a rewarding career choice. But times have changed, and while many of us might aspire to work in a specific industry (or even the same company) for the majority of our career, the reality is of a growing shift towards more dynamic and varied career paths.[6] For all but a few, the job for life has disappeared.

While it can be beneficial to apply focus early, it is equally important to establish a range of adaptable and future-proofed qualities that will serve you well over a lifetime of career or job changes. These are attributes and characteristics that are central to who you are and what you stand for, and which will enable you to adapt and apply yourself to new working environments, roles and positions. As we saw earlier, curiosity in itself opens up new opportunities, but also increases the scope for new knowledge and experiences. For example, astute judgement and criticality can be applied to a broad range of disciplines and sectors. The ability to deploy these qualities or characteristics in new fields is fundamental to keeping your career options open.

6. Charles Handy reflects on the emergence of 'portfolio workers' who do not work within the confines of a single, permanent job, but instead apply their skills across a number of varied roles and organisations: C. Handy, *The Empty Raincoat: Making Sense of the Future* (London: Random House, 1995).

As discussed in Chapter 10, there has been a significant rise in the number of freelancers, co-workers, part-time workers, contractors and entrepreneurs, many of whom are working across multiple sectors and industries. As this becomes the norm, your skills also need to be transferable across numerous sectors.

Multi-layers and career mobility

If the notion of a job for life has become a distant concept, the need to stay in demand (and employable) is greater than ever. Many of us are now having to manage our careers with such precision that the frequency with which we review our prospects or change careers is happening at a more rapid rate.[7] From students to mid-career professionals and entrepreneurs, the importance of building multi-linked networks that have the potential to take us through multiple careers cannot be underestimated.

There are also growing numbers of individuals who are deploying their skills and expertise with employers and clients across a combination of sectors simultaneously, resulting in a more multifaceted portfolio. This is another competitive environment where it is, again, important to look beyond the remit of your own industry expertise and explore different areas where you may be able to apply your knowledge and skills, thus broadening your experience in various sectors.[8]

Beyond regular employability skills: the skill nucleus

As we saw in Chapter 7, it is easy to fall into the trap of using common terms and rhetoric simply because we are echoing what we know employers are looking for. Soft skills (or interpersonal skills) that are attractive to employers, prospective customers or clients include

7. Roger Trapp commented in the mid-1990s: 'Gone is the job for life ... Gone is the clear functional identity and the progressive rise in income and security ... Instead, there is a world of customers and clients, adding value, lifelong learning, portfolio careers, self-development and an overwhelming need to stay employable.' R. Trapp, 'No More Jobs for Life – They Went Out with the Milkround', *The Independent* (19 October 1995). Available at: http://www.independent.co.uk/student/career-planning/no-more-jobs-for-life--they-went-out-with-the-milkround-1578338.html.

8. Joanna Grigg comments on the portfolio career (a term coined by Charles Handy), stating: 'A portfolio career is one where we have an income from a number of sources, perhaps a number of jobs, or a job and a business, or any combination of activities.' J. Grigg, *Portfolio Working: A Practical Guide to Thriving in the Changing Workplace* (London: Kogan Page, 1997), p. 48.

being a team player, having a strong work ethic, flexibility, being able to problem solve, good communication, decision making and time management skills, leadership experience and an ability to work under pressure. While these are clearly indispensable qualities, they are too often de-contextualised through lack of applied examples, resulting in meaningless generalisations.

Consider what particular expertise you have that can communicate your individuality. Rather than looking at your entire range of skills, in a box-ticking sense, hone in on a small number of core skills: your skill nucleus. Augment these skills so they become an integral part of who you are, not just what is expected of you.

Here is an example of the skill nucleus you might find for a journalist, but the principle can be applied to almost any industry or sector:

**author, writer,
visual communicator,
entrepreneur/product developer,
multichannel storyteller/narrator/
social connector/community builder**

skill nucleus

soft/hard skills

technical skills, research and analysis, data management,
copy-editing, critical thinking, news judgement,
journalism ethics, real-time reporting, social media engagement,
collaboration, crowdsourcing, passion, blogging and web writing,
data journalism, video, audio, mapping and geotagging, software skills,
knowledge of world and current affairs, law, audience development skills

This provides an indicative illustration of how to go beyond soft and hard skills to establish a skill nucleus. The lower part of the triangle highlights skills, requirements or qualifications that form part of the job description. They are a given for what is required to perform the role. However, the skill nucleus identifies descriptors that define who you are rather than what you do. The hard and soft skills are integral to the skill nucleus, but its core function is to set you apart from your competitors.

So, discrete from what employers and prospective clients expect, your skill nucleus very much defines *you*. It is anchored by self-defined terms and/or frames that consolidate your prime attributes. It is worth investing time in exploring your soft and hard skill set to isolate your skill nucleus. As you do so, you may discover abilities that do not necessarily appear anywhere within your radar. This is where you can start to break ground, focusing on the defining factors that distinguish you from your competitors. These skills should not only be resilient to disruption but also be forward looking and future-proofed.

Skill projection

Defining your skill nucleus may not be enough if you work in certain rapidly changing industries. For you, this exercise may involve exploring your core skills further by applying them to new sectors that may be less saturated with individuals with similar abilities. This strategy is less focused on employability per se, and more about adopting a holistic approach to industries as a whole. What elements of your skill nucleus can sustain and drive your career in the long term?

This will force you to speculate on the future of your industry. For example, if your sector was impacted by massive change tomorrow, what one quality do you possess that you would be able to easily transfer to a new industry? You might also want to consider, if you happen to end up working in the same industry for the next ten years, what skill will have been your key defining quality.

Continuing with the example of journalism, here is how you might assess the wider market for your skill set:

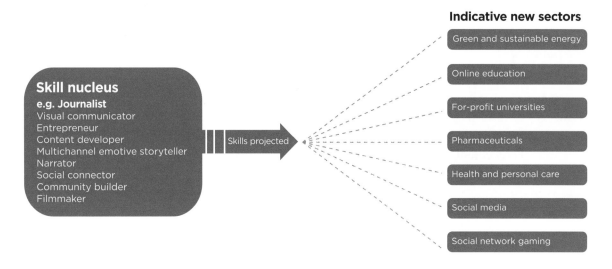

As you can see, the skills in the left-hand box become descriptors for what an employer might be looking for in an employee. The right-hand box lists new areas beyond the immediate profession. These are some of the fastest growing sectors where a journalist's skill nucleus could be applied successfully.[9]

So, how do you project your skills into unknown or unrelated areas to avoid skill disruption? If you are a qualified journalist, for instance, what business do you have delving into relatively unknown areas such as online education or green and sustainable energy? One approach is to address the connectivity between your networks and your experience (as described in Chapter 11). By gaining knowledge in these sectors, you will be able to pinpoint where collaboration has the potential to create

9. See R. Grant, 'The Seven Fastest Growing Industries of 2013' [infographic], Venture Beat (27 July 2013). Available at: http://venturebeat. com/2013/07/27/ the-7-fastest-growing-industries-of-2013-infographic/.

tangible value to you and the new sector. This will require an investment of your interest and time, as well as a genuine belief that you can add value. Another approach is to explore how collaboration with experts in those new sectors could yield opportunities and prospects in mutual exchanges of knowledge – for instance, talks, events or conferences.

Vision on the menu

Whenever I give talks to young designers, artists, photographers, illustrators and other creatives, it is always surprising during subsequent discussions how many of them are seeking employment and freelance opportunities in incredibly saturated environments. For a newly qualified design graduate, for example, the enticement of working for a top agency with a large profile is, of course, hugely attractive. But while many graduates are less selective, aiming for smaller companies where they can grow more organically, there still is a stubborn bottleneck of students all aiming for the same sector and the same roles.

I always explain that while it is fundamental to demonstrate ability and aptitude for the 'required skills', it is even more important to establish a core set of competences that (as the skill nucleus advocates) establishes new definitions of who they are and what they can do, but also has potential to go beyond what employers are looking for and expecting. This will open up additional areas in which to work, whether in employment or entrepreneurship.

Art and food integrated

I was recently looking through the portfolio of a young, dynamic MA fine art graduate who had finished her studies and was contemplating her next career move. She had an amazing collection of work, made up of a combination of personal projects and course assignments. She had already received some valuable career planning advice, but so had everyone else in her cohort. As a result, she was finding it difficult to locate the individuality that would set her apart from other artists who were on the same trajectory. My role was not to give her any more careers advice, but instead to look at areas where her personal expertise would be of value. I also introduced her to the idea of the connectivity equilibrium (see Chapter 11) and explained that she needed to achieve a balance of experiences and networks in order to increase her opportunities.

We agreed that she would take steps to getting some exposure outside of her field. Within a few months, she had secured some gallery space to exhibit her work. But what she did next really confirmed to me that she had truly grasped the principle of skill projection. What she hadn't told me at the time was that she was extremely passionate about cuisine, restaurants and interior design. If she hadn't taken up fine art, she would have most certainly been in the food business. So, rather than present her work immediately to the public, she had contacted interior designers who specialised in restaurant decor.

After months of collaborations on small projects, she was eventually hired as an artist and consultant-in-residence, advising on fine art installations that would be appropriate for food establishments. Of course, selling art in restaurants is nothing new. However, this strategy demonstrated this young woman's approach to looking beyond her immediate field in order to gain exposure and recognition for her work. And, of course, she is also averting future disruption to her skill nucleus by focusing on a wider sphere.

From skill projection to skill protection

- **Do not rely on your existing skills** – the world of work is changing rapidly. Arguably, what you know today is already out of date. The quest for innovation and new knowledge is not just valuable to you but also to your future employers and clients.

- **Open up opportunities** – do not sell your skills short by limiting your remit. Remember the portfolio workers who work beyond the confines of a single, permanent job. They apply their skills, abilities and qualities across a number of roles and organisations throughout their career.

- **Drop the list, find the nucleus** – if you are seeking your perfect role you will, of course, need to demonstrate a number of required skills to demonstrate that you are suitable. This streamlines the selection process for recruiters and employers. Nevertheless, it is important for *you* to focus on a set of core skills which might fall outside of mainstream requirements, but will define who you are: your skill nucleus.

- **Explore beyond your industry** – skill projection enables you to identify industries beyond your own where your skills might fit. Take a bold look at emerging and growing industries and understand how your expertise could bring value to that sector.

- **Avoid putting all your skills in one basket** – as we saw with the young artist, the interplay of two unrelated areas can lead to some very interesting and collaborative outcomes.

ReAct

1
Do not rely on
your existing
skills

2
Open up
opportunities

3
Drop the list,
find the nucleus

4
Explore
beyond your
industry

5
Avoid putting
all your skills in
one basket

18
The Unspoken Symphony

" *The appeal was instantaneous. It all seemed to click with an energy that was sublime, yet secured by a more reassured and affirmative combination of attraction and charm that all seemed to just make sense. She knew he might be the one. Her inner pragmatist and unconsciousness were aligned and, for once, in agreement. And yet, all of this without a single word spoken. The magnetism was beyond resistance and she felt compelled to make a move. Even though their eyes never met there was a connection. As she took a deep breath, she made her decision ...*

Steady. This is not the preamble to a romantic film or novel. Instead, it reveals certain factors that can be communicated instinctively, without requiring the spoken word, and which collectively form a tacit language – the 'unspoken symphony'. This is essentially what we transmit about ourselves through non-verbal or non-physical communication; it is inherently embedded in all our discourse, from introductory emails, proposals, bids and job applications to blogs, social media and websites. As this is the first impression that someone may get of us, we should consider very carefully what message we are transmitting.

You need to understand this unspoken communication in order to successfully harness opportunities, build networks, create communities and consolidate your identity. The combination of seven key elements of the unspoken symphony (belief, authenticity, knowledge, backstory, future story, time sensitivity and confidence) are those which, in my experience, other people are most responsive to when building connections and associations. More importantly, they also contribute to defining your individuality and character.[1]

Beyond the nucleus

In the previous chapter, we explored the skill nucleus as a way of refining the soft and hard skills required by employers and business

1. The unspoken symphony is a collective group of transmitted elements and patterns that I have observed in business leaders, entrepreneurs, creative graduates, students and colleagues throughout my career in the creative industries. The majority of these elements are communicated through non-verbal or non-physical contact. It also stems from the elements that I, personally, have felt it necessary to communicate and that have been pivotal in differentiating me in both my academic and professional practice.

associates to further define who you are and what you do. The unspoken symphony also enables you to effectively communicate your skill nucleus. How this is done will become clearer as each symphony is unravelled.

The seven elements can best be described as the indicators and qualities that help us to build assurances and connect effectively with an audience – often without saying a word. And this is not about body language or gestures either. The intrinsic factors of the unspoken symphony are natural and true to you; they are ingrained in your communication and presence. Well managed, your unspoken symphony can generate genuine connectivity with your audience.

Words beyond the inbox vortex

The unspoken symphony is made up of the following elements:

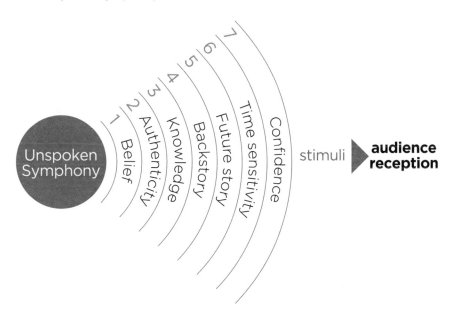

We will now explore each of the seven elements in more detail.

1. Belief – transmit it

A good starting point is to have an unbreakable belief in who you are and what you do. Having genuine confidence in your goals and dreams requires regular and consistent questioning of your objectives to ensure that you are still connecting with your purpose. Be your own devil's advocate: getting past constructive criticism and defending your purpose convincingly can strengthen your belief. Furthermore, you can't expect other people to endorse what you are doing if the belief does not start with you. Crossing the threshold of self-belief is a huge undertaking, but it is also incredibly rewarding.

2. Authenticity – project your own natural voice

Most definitions of authenticity include originality and genuineness. Your communication needs to transmit qualities and expertise that are undeniably true to who you are. While there can be a temptation to embellish for good effect, it is wise to steer clear of clever spin or rhetoric that may in any way discredit you. It is important to convey *your* natural voice and not that of others. A natural style that reflects who you are is all you need to convey your purpose and passion.

3. Knowledge – show it

Know your industry well, but make sure that you can back up your opinions and beliefs. Confidence is great, but it means little if your views are weak or unsubstantiated. You should also demonstrate a willingness to be open to new information. The ability to research, process and implement new knowledge implies an evolutionary mindset that is receptive to change.

4. Backstory – look back with pride

Your past achievements can help to communicate your objectives
for the future, so acknowledge key points in your backstory and past
experiences (e.g. cultural, academic, professional, social) that are
aligned with your current goals. While your backstory can help to define
you, it can also communicate how you might solve problems or meet
challenges in the future.

5. Future story – share a vision

Past achievements are vital in authenticating your qualities and
achievements, but you must also be able to demonstrate a forward-
looking vision. Your future story conveys both where you want to be and
that you have a resourceful mindset with one eye on the future. Your
future story can be daring, risk taking and ambitious, but remember
that you are asking other people to share in your vision. Venturing into
unknown and untested territory will require a lot of trust in you, so make
sure you create genuine connections and empathy.

6. Time sensitivity – good timing

Sensitive timing is crucial when you are making initial contact with an
audience. You should be realistic that what you are offering may not
be appropriate at that moment in time or that your approach may
not be aligned with the immediate needs of your recipients. However,
demonstrating an awareness of this, as well as flexibility about working
within an open time frame, can be extremely helpful when initiating
contact. Acknowledging potential barriers and working them to your
advantage can open up future possibilities (but make sure your research
is thorough and your knowledge is sound).

7. Confidence – know your authority

The distinctive combination of belief, authenticity, knowledge, backstory, future story and time sensitivity are contributory factors to your confidence, authority and tone. The ability to convey all these elements confidently will enhance the trust and conviction that others have in you.[2]

In summary, the seven elements of the unspoken symphony are vital non-verbal components that you transmit in all your communication. As effective stimuli, they not only help to define you, your purpose and objectives, but also help to increase the confidence others have in you to make intelligent and informed decisions.

The unspoken symphony is not set in stone. The elements are organic, so not all of them will be relevant to you, your ideas or objectives at all times. You may choose to explore different elements and build them into your own symphony. For example, if humour is an important element of your communication and a stimulus that people respond to, then delve into it further, figure out what works and then use it to maximum effect.

Flick the right switches

- **Consider the elements** – think about the seven key elements of the unspoken symphony and consider their role in your non-verbal communication (e.g. email, blogs, video). Constantly review these elements so that they truly communicate who you are and what you do.

- **Be mindful of audience** – be aware of what your audience will respond to positively and work towards delivering it. However, this should not be contrived or simply developed to fit their expectations.

2. Amanda Vickers and Steve Bavister suggest that when you are confident, 'you appear natural to others, they feel safe in your hands, and they believe in what you say more readily. Because you are more assertive this means they are more likely to buy your idea or products and implement your plans.' A. Vickers and S. Bavister, *Impact: Impress Your Way to Success* (Harlow: Pearson Education, 2011), p. 4.

- **Organic growth to suit you** – the unspoken symphony is not definitive and can be organic. You or your brand will have other tailor-fitted qualities and attributes that you will wish to communicate.

- **Audience awareness** – the unspoken symphony is of little value if you are communicating to the wrong audience. You should know exactly what you want to say and then ensure that your modes of communication are appropriate.

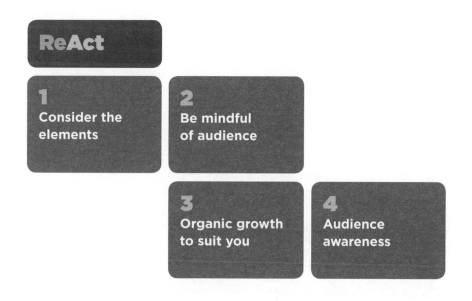

ReAct

1 Consider the elements

2 Be mindful of audience

3 Organic growth to suit you

4 Audience awareness

19
The Invisible Treasure Box

It is easy to be oblivious to the hidden treasures that surround us on an everyday basis. While these are not always apparent due to ordinary distractions, more often than not, we don't see the value or true worth in those things that are most immediate to us, such as our environment and place of work through to people we interact with, including colleagues, endorsers, family, friends and even critics who perform the role of devil's advocate, who make effective contributions to our careers and personal success.

Regardless of what stage we are at in our career, the key is recognising and having the ability to see the virtues of those in our networks and communities. We also need to be ultra-alert to what may be distracting us from the really important things. By not being present in the moment, or being otherwise preoccupied, we can sometimes become blinkered or unaware of situations as they are happening in real time; we are physically present but our mind is elsewhere.

Max and the invisible treasure box

This is the tale of a budding businessman and the invisible treasure box.

Max was a promising entrepreneur and self-confessed geek with a degree in computer science. He was a serial ideas generator, and his latest venture involved the development of a social media and mobile app. He had invested much time and energy into establishing his innovative concept and, although it was still in the very early stages, it appeared to be generating some interest among his community of collaborators, focus groups, network of acquaintances, colleagues, friends and supporters.

He was an avid and highly enthusiastic observer and blogger of the latest trends in social, digital and mobile applications. But there seemed to be an obstruction that was stopping him from committing to this particular project. He would put his idea on the back burner for months at a time and fail to make any significant progress. Something was preventing him from taking the key steps and progressing his business idea to the next stage. The obstacle was not financial because outlay was fairly minimal at this stage.

Max's idea had been through various stages of development, but it was still in pre-beta-preliminary-not-quite-ready-to-release-to-the-world status. Although enthusiastic and highly curious about developments in app technology and products, Max was also fixated on the success of other similar products, brands and services, such that it appeared to de-focus his own objectives. He felt compelled to hold off on his idea if he felt it could be improved on. But procrastination was not his problem either.

He was conscious of the feedback and attention his idea was gaining from people in his network, but he would often ignore these indicators. His real problem was a combination of blinkeredness and ignorance. Consequently, he failed to harness the value of his own achievements and instead focused on the successes of others, thus halting his own progress. His support network was more valuable than he had given it credit for.

Max's different time zone

In many respects, Max was operating in an alternative time zone from his network. Rich resources were available to him, from individuals and from his community, but he was unable to tap into it. His visions were set so far ahead that he was unable to see the hidden treasures that surrounded him in the present.

- Had Max been more vigilant and in the moment he would have noticed the genuine interest that others identified in his concept. So much so that they were willing to contribute time and expertise to help develop the idea. But he was locked into the achievements of his competitors and saw any advice as a hindrance rather than a support.

- Had Max been more attentive he would have seen the value in his long-time friend who, although not connected with social media, had an astute understanding of marketing and constantly probed him on questions that would have had a profound impact on the direction of his business.

- Had Max been less ignorant he would not have gazed over the shoulders of the young business consultants and branding experts who could advise him on business support en route to market.

- Had Max listened more intently to the people who were essentially going to be his customers, he would not have ignored their offer to test the beta versions of his application. Instead he had his eye on similar successful products that were selling at a premium.

Focus is a valuable asset when developing any concept, as is having an awareness of competing products or services. However, it also pays to be sensitive to the resources available to you. Max frequented a co-working space where there was a diverse and dynamic community of individuals working in similar fields. However, despite the collaborative culture that Max had access to, he usually preferred to work in isolation. Had he been more visible in this arena, the community within which he was working would also have discovered the treasure in his ideas.

All of these elements were open and available to Max; they were present and in the moment. But for Max they were hidden treasures that he did not see as part of his immediate world and consequently remained out of sight.

It is important that your receptors are open not only to the value in other people but also to the value that other people have *right now*, not in retrospect. So, how can you tap into the real value of those around you?

Present state awareness

It is vital to be engaged with factors that surround you in the present moment. Being aware of current circumstances as they happen – more commonly known as mindfulness – involves being in sync and fully receptive to people, resources and environments, and truly connecting with those elements in meaningful ways.

Whether you are developing a business concept or just starting out in your career, it is important to understand the difference between being observant and fully acknowledging the treasure around you. Raising your present state awareness is not a passive act; it requires you to be receptive and responsive to others. It is essential to have a forward-looking vision, but present state awareness acknowledges the importance of the factors around you now that can contribute towards your future vision.

It is all too common to look back in hindsight and wish that you had been able to connect on a deeper level with the resources, colleagues or processes that were available to you, or wish you had made the best out of those opportunities at the time. Present state awareness requires ultra-sensitivity, ultra-consciousness and ultra-attentiveness: being mindful of current events, engaging with your senses, listening intently, concentrating and observing in the present.[1]

The other side of the treasure box

As well as focusing on harnessing and appreciating the treasure in your midst, it is equally important that you, your ideas or your business are appreciated for their true worth. Whether you are developing a business concept or building your career, the treasure you create should be visible to your audience. This involves remaining on the radar of decision makers and staying relevant and knowledgeable.

1. Social theorist and psychologist, Mihaly Csikszentmihalyi, is best known for his research into the study of creativity and happiness. Among his numerous articles and publications is his seminal title, *Flow: The Psychology of Optimal Experience* (New York: HarperCollins, 1990). According to Csikszentmihalyi, there are numerous composite factors to 'flow', including strong concentration, focused attention and complete focus on the activity in the present moment.

In summary, it is vital to develop an acute awareness of the hidden treasures, such as support networks, that can make a difference to your ideas and professional development. These resources are not always immediately apparent and it requires sensitivity to appreciate their value in the present moment. Insight might come from the criticality of a devil's advocate, from failing and learning an important lesson or sensing new opportunities from an amalgam of your networks and experiences.

Discover your treasure

- **Stop and pause** – whether you are developing a business concept or are at the start of your career, consider the qualities of the people in your circle who could have a positive impact on your objectives and vision.

- **Not just people but space** – don't be oblivious to the value of your environment. Be aware, be observant and be responsive.

- **Exhibit your treasure** – whether you have been in a role for years, overlooked for promotion, developing a business concept or are entering the job market, ensure that your audience is aware of your qualities *now* – in retrospect is usually too late. Check that they are communicating back in real time so you know that your message is getting through.

- **Spread your treasure** – make your skills, virtues and qualities available to as broad an audience as possible so that you are in as many treasure boxes as possible. This involves not only communicating what you do but also how your qualities can be of real benefit to others.

ReAct

1
Stop and pause

2
Not just people but space

3
Exhibit your treasure

4
Spread your treasure

20
You:Optimised

Throughout this book, we have explored a range of factors, strategies and approaches that are essential in the process of rebranding and differentiating yourself. It would, however, be remiss of me to discuss professional development, rebranding, reinvention or personal change without looking at some of the important elements that support and facilitate such changes.

In this final chapter, we will look at the significance of being in good shape in terms of mindset, attitude and health, so that we are fully optimised ahead of any career or business opportunities. We will explore the notion of sustaining optimisation and how this can contribute to peak performance.

While well-being and health underpin the main discussion, the real focus is on long-term gain and optimisation to support personal and professional development, employment and business opportunities.

Five-a-life

Most people agree that well-being is made up of five essential components: career, social, financial, physical and community.[1] In this chapter, we will focus on the two areas of well-being that are most relevant to professional development – career well-being and physical well-being. However, it is always important to look beyond the threshold of short-term gain and look to supporting your career and business opportunities over longer periods.[2]

There is a wealth of resources about achieving a healthy lifestyle, although information on how this advice can be put into action and, furthermore, sustained over longer periods, is more scarce. The long-term commitment to a healthy diet, fitness, career development, relationships and finances is usually more challenging than initially starting the activity.[3]

1. Tom Rath and Jim Harter provide an overview of what contributes to well-being over a lifetime in *Wellbeing: The Five Essential Elements* (New York: Gallup Press, 2010).

2. Rath and Harter suggest that 'the single biggest threat to our own wellbeing tends to be ourselves ... We allow our short-term decisions to override what's best for our long-term wellbeing ... But the reality is, our short-term self still wins ... despite objections from our long-term self' (ibid., pp. 7–8).

3. Research for the *Journal of Clinical Psychology* produced by the University of Scranton in the United States revealed that nearly 45% of the interviewees made New Year's resolutions with only 8% being successful in achieving their resolution by the end of the year. See: http://www.statisticbrain. com/new-years-resolution-statistics/.

Obtaining that elusive work–life balance is something that most of us aspire to but few achieve. To ensure that all the spinning plates have your attention, and in a way that is manageable, you need to cultivate a plural mindset rather than splitting up your time and attention. When there are lots of factors competing for your attention, it is essential to prioritise and make clear distinctions between those that are distractions and those that are beneficial to you.

Right place – wrong time

Our final tale comes from Blake, who was in the right place but at the wrong time. Blake had a career in marketing. As a young, dynamic marketing executive he was relatively successful, on top of his game in his work and respected among his peers. He was also professional and knowledgeable – the 'go to' person in his company for intelligence. He was well connected and had a large network of associates from his industry and other interconnected fields.

However, Blake was unfulfilled in his work and, despite a couple of promotions in the same company over the years, he was considering a career move – a change of job and firm. He aspired to work with a large digital communications company and had done his research – from the kind of projects they undertook to the internal business infrastructure. He was planning to make an approach to the company shortly.

He improved his professional profile and updated his website, blog and portfolio. In order to stand out from the crowd, he also thought it would be a good idea to take a proactive approach by striking while the iron wasn't hot. He made contact with a number of individuals in the company and expressed interest in the work they were doing. He went to as many of their speaker events as possible and attended numerous networking events.

To avoid putting all his eggs in one basket, he multiplied his efforts and made contact with other organisations in similar fields where he also had an interest. His satellites and his tangible and intangible factors were active and busy working for him. For months he had made regular contact with companies and individuals, and was keeping a balanced log of 'straight rejection' and 'generic responses'. Still, nothing promising, and he grew increasingly frustrated. Nevertheless, he persisted.

One day, after what seemed like a lifetime, his persistence paid off. The original company he had taken an interest in took notice – he had finally appeared on their radar. One of the creative directors asked him to come in for a meeting. Perfect. All the elements were in place. Sharp portfolio, sharp profile, sharp shoes. But as finely tuned as all these things appeared, and regardless of all the positive, well-managed and developed elements that supported his illustrious career, Blake had disregarded one of the most important factors – time.

He made the awful mistake of turning up for his meeting just two minutes late! Two minutes were all it took to convince the creative director that perhaps Blake hadn't taken this opportunity seriously enough. Two minutes were enough time for the creative director to decide that being late was sufficient to cancel one of the most important meetings of Blake's career before he had even arrived. An opportunity lost and a major lesson learned. Despite having all the elements in place, he had taken his eye off the one spinning plate that really mattered – timekeeping.

It is common to encounter individuals, like Blake, who have lots of positive and encouraging factors in place, yet drop the ball at the last minute. Being optimised means adopting a holistic outlook on *all* the elements that contribute to you achieving your best and, most importantly, ensuring that they are also deployed to full effect when it really matters.

In it for the long run

Apply strategies and methods that will have a long-term impact on your career or professional development as opposed to quick fixes. While many of the approaches discussed in this book require immediate engagement, there is no magic wand. The benefits will only come if they are applied consistently, thereby resulting in sustainable and manageable change.

This is about more than just a change of practice or lifestyle. It requires regular self-reflection and introspection to ensure that you are continuing to maintain your objectives. For example, it would be pointless to nurture your network but to fall back into a pattern of accumulating large numbers of inactive contacts, or to develop an awareness of over-used words and terminologies only to see them creep back into your regular vocabulary.

From the eyes of the professionals

To provide a wider context on the importance of optimal performance, I interviewed a number of experienced professionals from some diverse fields. I wanted to explore optimisation with them, as well as other elements that contribute to peak performance. I also wanted to discover what drives them and how this can be sustained in the long term in their personal and professional lives.

The start-up coach

Marie Milligan is a highly regarded coach, educator and writer who specialises in the development of innovative start-ups and the wellness of entrepreneurs. Living a 'slow' life on a canal boat in Little Venice, Marie shares her views on why wellness propels creativity and how it optimises life and business.

Creative, entrepreneurial people often juggle many things simultaneously and strive to reach big goals fast. They have this inherent mindset compelling them to press on and take action. As creative-doers and reflective-thinkers, their mind incessantly creates new ideas, mulls over old ones and scans info constantly. In the worst cases, this pressure to reach successful goals brings the risk of burning out. If overworked or under pressure, our batteries flash warning signs that tell us they need to be recharged. However, there's an innate fear that if we do switch off or slow down, we'll somehow fall behind, lose work and damage our reputation.

For me, the Slow Movement, which encourages us to slow down life's pace and be more mindful, has energised me, not held me back. Living at a pace that feels comfortable, with a values-centred compass, can help you to lead your mission with more vigour and from your centre.

Our entrepreneurial culture focuses so much on 'the doing', but balance and fulfilment comes from allowing space for just 'being' too. Our mind, body and soul system constantly demand moments of rest. It inspires our creativity; we start to think afresh, are more in tune with ourselves and find new solutions to old challenges. The Healthy Entrepreneur wellness programme and ebook I devised came from needing to empower the change-makers to be and do the extraordinary but in a self-caring, sustainable way. 'Healthy' implies optimum nutrition and fitness but it's also about a mind-body-soul that feels in tune.

It's about:

• Resonance, positive energy and mindset.

• Maintaining a curious attitude to life.

- A desire to create or contribute.

- Taking the risk to be vulnerable and open-hearted, learning to self-express and approach life with an easy step.

For entrepreneurs and anyone else starting out in business or other career opportunities, it's also about ensuring that you have the right tools and systems in place to enable you to take that break readily, without fear or regret.

The filmmaker

Sasha Damjanovski is an award-winning filmmaker, director, writer and producer. Among his projects are the films, *Defining Fay* and *Dance with Me*. He shares his views on his approach to his work, as well as methods that help him to grow and keep him motivated and optimised professionally and personally, while also maintaining a sense of gratification and fulfilment in his career.

Prior to any project, it's important to get an understanding of why, what and how. I have to know 'why' I'm doing something, whether it's a creative challenge, career advancement, financial gain or experiment. This purpose helps me to stay focused, motivated, enthusiastic and happy to be working on a project, even when the conditions are tough or the reward uncertain.

The 'what' is about evaluating whether a particular project is going to serve my purpose. If my purpose or 'why' is financial gain, then making an ingeniously creative short film for no money isn't necessarily a good idea. I will then consider the 'how' – such as how the project will be financed or managed. At this stage, a well-devised plan of action, supported by research, drives and sustains the motivation.

I also find it essential to continuously re-evaluate. In our lives and careers, we change and things around us change. Things that mattered to me once may not matter to me today, and if my purpose has changed, I'll need different challenges and rewards from my work. I equally need to re-evaluate my resources and ability – what seemed impossible last year suddenly may have become achievable because of changes in the market, advances in technology, trends and so on. Re-evaluating involves having a frank and objective dialogue with myself.

Another factor that continues to influence and motivate me is my interest in process – for example, how a particular film got to be made, how it was pitched and marketed, who financed it, what compromises were made to get it to the screen and any new methods in the film that may inform my own work. These are just some of the factors that continuously drive, motivate and keep me enthused throughout the stages of my career.

The health and fitness expert

Dan Roberts is a leading figure in the international fitness community, with a distinctly holistic philosophy. His group of companies delivers world-class fitness and well-being coaching for a wide range of clients, including business leaders, public figures, actors, models and sports teams.

Lifestyle coaching and optimal nutrition are among some of the essential elements that help people to reach their goals but, more importantly, stay there. I believe we are all 'athletes', and adopting the mindset is vital to staying relatively optimised – feeling athletic, healthy and living in total harmony with your body.

There are three key essentials that, personally and professionally, I believe directly affect our body's ability to perform at its peak and also maintenance in the long term: exercise, nutrition and sleep.

- Exercise – our body's natural state is to be agile, strong and fit. Our muscular and cardiovascular systems are designed to adapt to various conditions, from everyday activities to intensive workouts. Engaging in regular activities that keep us moving both physically and mentally is paramount to living healthily and optimally, ensuring the mind and body perform and function as one.

- Nutrition – you probably do not need to be reminded of the importance of a good diet. What is worth pointing out, however, is attitude. Our attitudes tend to shape our decisions, and those decisions eventually shape us, inside and out, both physically and mentally.

- Sleep – research has shown that if you are lacking sleep and are relatively under-slept, this can have an impact on metabolism and hormone levels. So, sleep is not just essentially for mental alertness; the physical benefits are also evident.

These key factors are essential in our personal and professional lives. The most effective way of staying motivated is to get results. Seeing results can also provide a psychological boost. The importance of these factors cannot be underestimated and they are in many ways the operating systems that enable you to perform at your best.

Stay tuned

- **Don't wave a magic wand** – many of the methods and approaches discussed in this book require a longer term attitude and consistent and regular application of the strategies and techniques.

- **Stay balanced** – keeping those plates spinning isn't easy. Balancing the various elements in our lives is challenging, but it is important to prioritise to ensure that factors as valuable as time do not end up being obstacles.

- **Find your fuel** – we all have broad and diverse attitudes towards health, fitness and well-being. However, it is important to establish your level, find the things that work for you and keep you well-tuned and fuelled in order to sustain your objectives in the long term.

- **Re-evaluate** – ensure that you are constantly reassessing what inspires and enthuses you, with the understanding that as you change so do the things that keep you optimised and motivated.

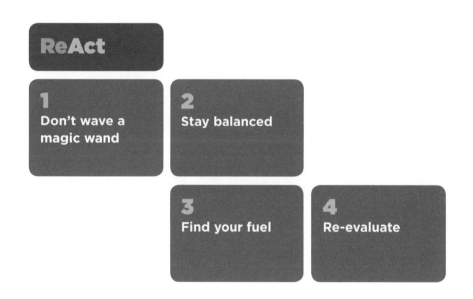

ReAct

1
Don't wave a
magic wand

2
Stay balanced

3
Find your fuel

4
Re-evaluate

Final words

Go forth and apply

We have reached the end of our journey. But it is very much just the beginning for you as you start to apply the new strategies, approaches and ways of thinking we have discussed to become more distinctive. The methods and approaches in this book work, but they also need you to be engaged and consistent in applying them. They have delivered proven results with individuals and businesses I have worked with in the past, many of whom have been kind enough to contact me after achieving their objectives, attributing, in part, their success and increase in opportunities to my strategies.

This book was also written for the future occupants, leaders, movers and shakers of roles and positions in sectors that may not even exist yet. While many of the references and examples relate to specific moments in the past, the methodologies are very much forward looking and, I hope, future-proof.

Whatever stage you are at in your career, you will undoubtedly be faced with new career challenges, new prospects or even new environments. If the predictions are true, automation and computerisation will continue to transform the industrial and economic landscape. How might this impact on the work you do now or in the future?

Although I have commented on the value of transferable skills and establishing your skill nucleus, I have also sought to explore the notion of future-proof skills which will enable you to transcend the threat of skill disruption. By continually self-assessing and applying the strategies and approaches discussed in this book, you will differentiate yourself sufficiently to equip yourself to meet the demands of a constantly changing working environment throughout your career.

Finally, I have endeavoured to provide signposts to other relevant references and material that you may find useful. Research further the individuals and organisations mentioned in this book and see what more you can discover that would support your own objectives.

I have one last task for you: please set two dates in your diary – one three months from now and the other six months from now – and write in the title of this book. As a self-reflective process, revisit the book at these intervals to see how many ideas and strategies you have applied, and consider how it has changed the way you think and do things differently. As you enter new territories and face different career challenges, keep applying the principles and approaches outlined in this book to ensure that you continue being seen, heard and noticed.

I wish you well in all stages of your on-going personal or professional development. As your story continues, it would please me immensely to know that some of the approaches, techniques and strategies have contributed to make positive changes in your career or business ideas.

Thank you for reading.

Now, go forth and apply.

Bibliography

Aitkenhead, D. (2012). 'Ozwald Boateng: Does My Head Look Big In This?', *The Guardian* (9 March). Available at: http://www.theguardian.com/fashion/2012/mar/09/ozwald-boateng-fashion-designer-tailor.

Arbesman, S. (2012). *The Half-Life of Facts: Why Everything Has An Expiration Date*. New York: Penguin.

Augustin, S. (2009). 'The Smell is Right – Using Scents to Enhance Life', *Psychology Today* (23 December). Available at: http://www.psychologytoday.com/blog/people-places-and-things/200912/the-smell-is-right-using-scents-enhance-life.

Barabba, V. P. (2011). *The Decision Loom: A Design for Interactive Decision-Making in Organizations*. Axminster: Triarchy Press.

Belsky, S. (2009). *Making Ideas Happen: Overcoming the Obstacles Between Vision and Reality*. New York: Penguin.

Bennett, D. (2013). 'Content Marketing Connects Brands with Target Audiences', *American Genius* (28 March). Available at: http://agbeat.com/business-marketing/content-marketing-connects-brands-with-target-audiences/.

Berkun, S. (2009). *The Myths of Innovation*. Sebastopol, CA: O'Reilly Media.

Biery, M. E. (2013). 'Industries to Watch in 2014: The 10 Fastest-Growing Fields', *Forbes* (29 December). Available at: http://www.forbes.com/sites/sageworks/2013/12/29/industries-to-watch-in-2014-the-10-fastest-growing-fields/.

Blanchard, K. and Spaulding, T. (2010). *It's Not Just Who You Know: Transforming Your Life*. New York: Crown Publishing.

Boduch, R. (n.d.). *Online Copywriting Secrets: 170+ Quick Tips for Making All Your Web Sales Copy More Compelling, Convincing and Responsive*. Kindle edition.

BOP Consulting (2010). *Mapping the Creative Industries: A Toolkit* (Creative and Cultural Economy Series 2). London: British Council. Available at: http://creativeconomy.britishcouncil.org/media/uploads/files/English_mapping_the_creative_industries_a_toolkit_2-2.pdf.

Brown, R. (2007). *How to Build Your Reputation: The Secrets of Becoming the 'Go To' Professional in a Crowded Marketplace*. Penryn: Ecademy Press.

Byrant, A. (2009). 'He Prizes Questions More Than Answers' [interview with Tim Brown], *New York Times* (24 October). Available at: http://www.nytimes.com/2009/10/25/business/25corner.html?pagewanted=all.

Campbell, A. (2013). 'Number of Part-Time Young Workers on the Rise in the UK', *BBC Newsbeat* (20 February). Available at: http://www.bbc.co.uk/newsbeat/21512615.

Cardillo, E. R., Watson, C. E., Schmidt, G. L., Kranjec, A. and Chatterjee, A. (2012). 'From Novel to Familiar: Tuning the Brain for Metaphors', *Neuroimage* 59(4): 3212–3221. Available at: http://www.ncbi.nlm.nih.gov/pmc/articles/PMC3288556/.

Casserly, M. (2012). 'The 10 Skills That Will Get You Hired in 2013', *Forbes* (10 December) Available at: http://www.forbes.com/sites/meghancasserly/2012/12/10/the-10-skills-that-will-get-you-a-job-in-2013/.

Casserly, M. (2012). 'Dream Companies for the Class of 2012: Everybody Wants to Work at Google', *Forbes* (11 May). Available at: http://www.forbes.com/sites/meghancasserly/2012/05/11/dream-companies-for-class-2012-everybody-wants-to-work-at-google/.

Champy, J. (2008). *Outsmart! How to Do What Your Competitors Can't*. Harlow: Financial Times/Prentice Hall.

Choi, C. (2013). 'Top 10 Overused LinkedIn Profile Buzzwords of 2013' [infographic], *LinkedIn Blog* (11 December). Available at: http://blog.linkedin.com/2013/12/11/buzzwords-2013/.

Csikszentmihalyi, M. (1990). *Flow: The Psychology of Optimal Experience*. New York: HarperCollins.

de Bono, E. (1990). *PO: Beyond Yes and No.* Harmondsworth: Penguin.

de Bono, E. (2009). *Six Thinking Hats*. London: Penguin.

Department for Business Innovation & Skills (2012). *Business Population Estimates for the UK and Regions 2012* (17 October). Available at: https://www.gov.uk/government/uploads/system/uploads/attachment_data/file/80247/bpe-2012-stats-release-4.pdf.

Di Salvo, D. (2013). '10 Reasons Why We Struggle With Creativity', *Forbes* (16 March). Available at: http://www.forbes.com/sites/daviddisalvo/2013/03/16/10-reasons-why-we-struggle-with-creativity/2/.

Dickler, J. (2009). 'The Hidden Job Market', *CNN Money* (10 June). Available at: http://money.cnn.com/2009/06/09/news/economy/hidden_jobs/.

Dishman, L. (2013). 'The Future of Coworking and Why It Will Give Your Business a Huge Edge', *Fast Company* (15 January). Available at: http://www.fastcompany.com/3004788/future-coworking-and-why-it-will-give-your-business-huge-edge.

Dunbar, R. (2010). *How Many Friends Does One Person Need? Dunbar's Number and Other Evolutionary Quirks*. London: Faber and Faber.

Edwards, A. P., Edwards, C., Wahl, S. T. and Myers, S. A. (2012). *The Communication Age, Connecting and Engaging*. Thousand Oaks, CA: SAGE.

Enders, A. (2008). 'The Importance of Place: Where Writers Write and Why', *Poets & Writers* (March/April). Available at: http://www.pw.org/content/importance_place_where_writers_write_and_why_0?cmnt_all=1.

Foertsch, C. (2013). '4.5 New Coworking Spaces Per Work Day', *deskmag* (4 March). Available at: http://www.deskmag.com/en/2500-coworking-spaces-4-5-per-day-741.

Frey, C. B. and Osborne, M. A. (2013). 'The Future of Employment: How Susceptible Are Jobs to Computerisation?' (17 September). Available at: http://www.oxfordmartin.ox.ac.uk/downloads/academic/The_Future_of_Employment.pdf.

Goddard, J. and Eccles, T. (2013). *Uncommon Sense, Common Nonsense: Why Some Organisations Consistently Outperform Others*. London: Profile Books.

Godin, S. (2007). *Small is the New Big! And 183 Other Riffs, Rants and Remarkable Business Ideas*. New York: Penguin.

Godin, S. (2010). *Linchpin: Are You Indispensable? How to Drive Your Career and Create a Remarkable Future*. London: Piatkus.

Graham, H. (2008). 'Why So Many Start-ups Fail', *BBC News* (11 December). Available at: http://news.bbc.co.uk/1/hi/business/7759207.stm.

Grant, R. (2013). 'The Seven Fastest Growing Industries of 2013' [infographic], *Venture Beat* (27 July). Available at: http://venturebeat.com/2013/07/27/the-7-fastest-growing-industries-of-2013-infographic/.

Greenslade, R. (2013). 'How Digital Revolution Gives Power to the People', *London Evening Standard* (6 November). Available at: http://www.standard.co.uk/business/media/roy-greenslade-how-digital-revolution-gives-power-to-the-people-8924261.html.

Grigg, J. (1997). *Portfolio Working: A Practical Guide to Thriving in the Changing Workplace*. London: Kogan Page.

Groom, B. (2013). 'Homeworker Numbers Rise 13% in Five Years, Despite Recession', *ft.com* (17 May). Available at: http://www.ft.com/cms/s/0/8411e8a4-be2b-11e2-9b27-00144feab7de.html#ixzz2Tf3eD5VD.

Handy, C. (1995). *The Empty Raincoat: Making Sense of the Future*. London: Random House.

Hertz, N. (2013). *Eyes Wide Open: How to Make Smart Decisions in a Confusing World*. London: William Collins.

Hesselbein, F. and Goldsmith, M. (2009). *The Organization of the Future: Visions, Strategies, and Insights on Managing in a New Era*. San Francisco, CA: Jossey-Bass.

Holbrook Hernandez, J. (2010). 'Is Your Resume Plagued with Overused Resume Terms?', *Career Rocketeer* (14 September). Available at: http://careerrocketeer.com/2010/09/is-your-resume-plagued-with-overused-resume-terms.html.

Howkins, J. (2001). *The Creative Economy: How People Make Money from Ideas*. London: Penguin.

Huhman, H. (2013). '6 Reasons People Leave Big Companies to Join Startups', *Tech Cocktail* (1 June). Available at: http://tech.co/6-reasons-people-leave-big-companies-to-join-startups-2013-06.

Ifould, R. (2013). 'Curiosity: The Secret to Your Success', *Psychologies* (16 January). Available at: http://www.psychologies.co.uk/self/curiosity-the-secret-to-your-success.html.

Ipsos MORI (2012). 'Fifty Shades of Opportunity' (14 September). Available at: http://www.ipsos-mori.com/newsevents/ca/1171/Fifty-Shades-of-Opportunity.aspx.

Jacobs, K. (2013). 'UK Freelance Economy Booming, Research Finds', *HR Magazine* (23 August). Available at: http://www.hrmagazine.co.uk/hro/news/1078168/uk-freelance-economy-booming-research#sthash.3o4Ppmv6.dpuf.

Jiwa, B. (2012). *Make Your Idea Matter: Stand Out with a Better Story*. N.p.: Story of Telling Press.

John, O. P. and Srivastava, S. (1999). 'The Big-Five Trait Taxonomy: History, Measurement and Theoretical Perspectives', University of California at Berkeley. Available at: http://pages.uoregon.edu/sanjay/pubs/bigfive.pdf.

Kashdan, T. (2009). *Curious? Discover the Missing Ingredient to a Fulfilling Life*. New York: HarperCollins.

Kashdan, T. (2010). 'The Power of Curiosity', *Experience Life* (May). Available at: http://experiencelife.com/article/the-power-of-curiosity/.

Keen, A. (2010). 'Simon Waldman on Creative Disruption', *Harvard Business Review Blog Network* (2 December). Available at: http://blogs.hbr.org/2010/12/simon-waldman-on-creative-disr/.

Kiss, J. (2013). 'Kevin Systrom, Instagram's Man of Vision, Now Eyes Up World Domination', *The Guardian* (11 October). Available at: http://www.theguardian.com/technology/2013/oct/11/instagram-kevin-systrom-world-domination.

Knabb, C. (2010). '10 Reasons Why Most Demo Recordings are Rejected', *Music Biz Academy* (April). Available at: http://www.musicbizacademy.com/knab/articles/10demosrejected.htm.

Kohrman, M (2003). '9 Easy-to-Steal Habits of the Super Successful', *Fast Company* (25 July). Available at: http://www.fastcompany.com/3014736/how-to-be-a-success-at-everything/9-easy-to-steal-habits-of-the-super-successful.

Kreamer, A. (2012). 'The Rise of Coworking Office Spaces', *Harvard Business Review Blog Network* (19 September). Available at: http://blogs.hbr.org/2012/09/the-rise-of-co-working-office/.

Krotoski, A. (2010). 'Robin Dunbar: We Can Only Ever Have 150 Friends At Most ...', *The Observer* (14 March). Available at: http://www.theguardian.com/technology/2010/mar/14/my-bright-idea-robin-dunbar.

Lehrer, J. (2012). *Imagine: How Creativity Works*. New York: Canongate Books.

Lesyk, J. J. (1998). 'The Nine Mental Skills of Successful Athletes', *Ohio Center for Sport Psychology*. Available at: http://www.sportpsych.org/nine-mental-skills-overview.

Levitt, T. (2002). 'Creativity is Not Enough', *Harvard Business Review*. Available at: http://hbr.org/2002/08/creativity-is-not-enough/ar/1.

Linkner, J. (2012). 'Your New Job: Disruptor', *Forbes* (26 March). Available at: http://www.forbes.com/sites/joshlinkner/2012/03/26/your-new-job-disruptor/.

Litchfield, D. (2012). 'Big Company or Start-Up – Which is the Best Option for You?', *The Independent* (6 October). Available at: http://www.independent.co.uk/student/young-entrepreneurs/big-company-or-startup--which-is-the-best-option-for-you-7998725.html.

Llopis, G. (2009). *Earning Serendipity: Four Skills for Creating and Sustaining Good Fortune in Your Work*. Austin, TX: Greenleaf Book Group.

Llopis, G. (2011). 'What We Can All Learn from Amazon about Seeing Business Opportunities Others Don't See', *Forbes* (7 February). Available at: http://www.forbes.com/sites/glennllopis/2011/02/07/what-we-can-all-learn-from-amazon-about-seeing-business-opportunities-others-dont-see/.

Locke, G. and Gavin, F. (2011). *Export: Five Keys to Entering New Markets*. Singapore: John Wiley & Sons.

Magsamen, S. (2009). 'How to Embrace Your Inner Child', *Oprah* (27 October). Available at: http://www.oprah.com/spirit/How-to-Embrace-Your-Inner-Child-Sandra-Magsamen.

Marketing Magazine (2012). 'Media Starts to Catch Up with the Changing Consumer' (16 October). Available at: http://www.marketingmagazine.co.uk/article/1154781/media-starts-catch-changing-consumer.

McGrath, F. (2013). 'Small is Big and Job Satisfaction', *Financial News* (3 October). Available at: http://www.efinancialnews.com/story/2013-03-10/financial-news-job-satisfaction-survey-small-is-beautiful?ea9c8a2de0ee111045601ab04d673622.

McRae, R. and John, O. P. (1992). *An Introduction to the Five-Factor Model and its Applications*. Upper Saddle River, NJ: Prentice Hall.

Morgan, A. (2009). *Eating the Big Fish: How Challenger Brands Can Compete Against Brand Leaders* (2nd edn). Hoboken, NJ: John Wiley & Sons.

Nahai, N. (2012). *Webs of Influence: The Psychology of Online Persuasion*. Harlow: Pearson Education.

Pallotta, D. (2011). 'Stop Thinking Out of the Box', *Harvard Business Review Blog Network* (7 November).

Available at: http://blogs.hbr.org/pallotta/2011/11/stop-thinking-outside-the-box.html/.

Parkes, G. (2009). 'Jobs That No Longer Exist: 10 Industries Heading for Extinction', *Aol Jobs* (17 December). Available at: http://jobs.aol.com/articles/2009/12/17/10-industries-heading-for-extinction/.

Peiffer, V. (2002). *Positive Thinking: Everything You Have Always Known About Positive Thinking But Were Afraid to Put into Practice*. London: HarperCollins.

Pennington, R. (2013). *Make Change Work: Staying Nimble, Relevant, and Engaged in a World of Constant Change*. Hoboken, NJ: John Wiley & Sons.

Pink, D. (2010). 'How to Make Your Own Luck' [interview with Richard Wiseman], *Fast Company* (30 June). Available at: www.fastcompany.com/46732/how-make-your-own-luck.

Pink, D. (2011). *Drive: The Surprising Truth About What Motivates Us*. New York: Canongate Books.

Pollak, L. (2013). 'The Top Job Search Trends of 2013', *LinkedIn Blog* (14 January). Available at: http://blog.linkedin.com/2013/01/14/top-job-search-trends-2013/.

Porter, J. (2013). 'How Failure Made These Entrepreneurs Millions', *Entrepreneur* (14 June). Available at: http://www.entrepreneur.com/article/227011.

Prensky, M. (2001). 'Digital Natives, Digital Immigrants: Part 1', *On the Horizon* 9(5): 1–6.

Rajan, A. (2013). 'Be Creative If You Want to Outsmart the Robots', *London Evening Standard* (13 February). Available at: http://www.standard.co.uk/comment/amol-rajan-be-creative-if-you-want-to-outsmart-the-robots-9125649.html.

Rath, T. and Hartner, J. (2010). *Well-Being: The Five Essential Elements*. New York: Gallup Press.

Reinertsen, D. (2000). 'Try to Understand the Difference between Good and Bad Failures', *Electronic Design* (1 May). Available at: http://electronicdesign.com/archive/try-understand-difference-between-good-and-bad-failures.

Roberts, J. (2010). 'How to Increase Your Luck Surface Area', *Codus Operandi*. Available at: http://www.codusoperandi.com/posts/increasing-your-luck-surface-area.

Robinson, K. (2006). 'How Schools Kill Creativity' [video], *TED* (February). Available at: http://www.ted.com/talks/ken_robinson_says_schools_kill_creativity?language=en.

Rogers, E. M. (2003). *Diffusion of Innovations*. New York: Simon & Schuster.

Salter, C. (2007). 'Failure Doesn't Suck' [interview with James Dyson], *Fast Company* (1 May). Available at: http://www.fastcompany.com/59549/failure-doesnt-suck.

Schawbel, D. (2013). *Promote Yourself: The New Rules for Building an Outstanding Career*. London: Piatkus.

Schulz, K. (2011). 'On Being Wrong' [video], *TED* (March). Available at: http://www.ted.com/talks/kathryn_schulz_on_being_wrong?language=en.

Sebastian, M. (2012). 'The 10 Most Useless Buzzwords', *Entrepreneur* (20 December). Available at: http://www.entrepreneur.com/article/225310.

Sernovitz, A. (2012). *Word of Mouth Marketing: How Smart Companies Get People Talking*. Austin, TX: Greenleaf Book Group.

Sharma, R. S. (2004). *The Monk Who Sold His Ferrari*. London: HarperElement.

Sommer, C. (2012). 'Want to Become Known as an Industry Expert? 3 Tips to Get You Started', *Forbes*

(18 January). Available at: http://www.forbes.com/sites/carisommer/2012/01/18/want-to-become-known-as-an-industry-expert-3-tips-to-get-you-started/.

Stehr, N. and Grundmann, R. (2011). *Experts: The Knowledge and Power of Expertise*. Abingdon: Routledge.

Stringer, H. (2013). '10 CV Clichés to Avoid', *Warwick: The Careers Blog* (2 September). http://careersblog.warwick.ac.uk/2013/09/02/10-cv-cliches-to-avoid/.

Terdiman, D. (2013). 'Instagram's Systrom: We're "Not a Photography Company"', *CNET* (31 May). Available at: http://www.cnet.com/uk/news/instagrams-systrom-were-not-a-photography-company/.

Timewise Foundation (2013). 'The Flexibility Trap'. Available at: http://timewisefoundation.org.uk/wp-content/uploads/2013/07/Flexibility_Trap_-report.pdf.

Trapp, R. (1995). 'No More Jobs for Life – They Went Out with the Milkround', *The Independent* (19 October). Available at: http://www.independent.co.uk/student/career-planning/no-more-jobs-for-life--they-went-out-with-the-milkround-1578338.html.

Tyrangiel, J. (2007). 'Radiohead Says: Pay What You Want', *Time* (1 October). Available at: http://content.time.com/time/arts/article/0,8599,1666973,00.html#ixzz2igAxTLc1.

Vickers, A., Bavister, S. and Smith, J. (2011). *Impact: Impress Your Way to Success*. Harlow: Pearson Education.

Waldman, S. (2010). *Creative Disruption: What You Need to Do to Shake Up Your Business in a Digital World*. Harlow: Financial Times/Prentice Hall.

Walter, E. (2012). 'The Rise of Social Media', *Fast Company* (28 August). Available at: http://www.fastcompany.com/3000794/rise-visual-social-media.

Wheeler, A. (2012). *Designing Brand Identity: An Essential Guide for the Whole Branding Team* (4th edn). Hoboken, NJ: John Wiley & Sons.

Wiseman, R. (2003). 'The Luck Factor', *Skeptical Inquirer* (May/June). Available at: http://richardwiseman.files.wordpress.com/2011/09/the_luck_factor.pdf.

Wiseman, R. (2004). *The Luck Factor: The Scientific Study of the Luck Mind*. London: Arrow.

Wiseman, R. (2010). *59 Seconds: Think a Little, Change a Lot*. London: Macmillan.

Woods, C. (2013). *The Devil's Advocate: 100 Business Rules You Must Break*. Harlow: Pearson Education.

Working, R. (2011). '10 Overused Words on LinkedIn That Will Bury Your Résumé', *Ragan's PR Daily* (14 December). Available at: http://www.prdaily.com/Main/Articles/10_overused_words_on_LinkedIn_that_will_bury_your_10307.aspx#.

Zack, D. (2010). *Networking for People Who Hate Networking: A Field Guide for Introverts, the Overwhelmed, and the Underconnected*. San Francisco, CA: Berrett-Koehler.

Index

Acknowledgements

I would firstly like to thank God for helping me to make something out of the gift of creativity.

Thank you to my loving and wonderful wife, Glenda, for having great faith in me, supporting me and believing in everything I do. You are special way beyond words could ever say. Love always! To my beautiful daughters, Laney and Kiki – who bring me so much happiness and joy – it is incredible how much I continue to learn from you both. Love you …

←----------------------------- THIS MUCH!----------------------------------→

Thank you to my mum – you amaze and inspire me immensely with your energy. (Thanks for calling me almost every day to ask me how the book was going – it's finished now!) To my dear siblings, Jamie, Helen and Jason, for your care, love and support, and still making me do proper belly laughs about the silliest things! To my dad for providing me with strong principles from an early age. To my uncle, 'Big Daddy', who taught me very important lessons about business and life. To 'Swift' George for sharing your creative journey and entrepreneurship.

A very big thanks to everyone at Crown House Publishing, especially Caroline Lenton for seeing potential in me, helping me to find my voice and believing in me. A very big thanks to Ian Gilbert of Independent Thinking for being a huge inspiration and sharing my vision while providing invaluable expertise, insight and ideas in the development of this book. Thanks also to Louise Upton for helping me to craft and shape my words, to grow and be a better writer. I really could not have made it this far without you all.

Special thanks to Nathalie Nahai – my treasure box – as well as being a great friend, you have been incredibly generous with your time, guidance, advice and professional perspective.

Thanks also to: Martin Roach for being so supportive and helping me with my ideas over the years; Marie Milligan – you are so full of life – thanks for your encouragement; Sasha Damjanovski – thanks for your valuable time and sitting down with me over coffees to talk about the process and research for this book; and Dan Roberts for your incredible time and support despite your very busy schedule. Truly grateful.

A big thanks to my friends and colleagues who mean so much to me and, in numerous ways, have helped me throughout my career: Zaid Ali for being an incredible role model, great friend and advisor; Jude Oneyaka, a life-long friend, for sharing your creative passion and energy all these years; George Fearon for being a wonderful personal and family friend; Diana Donaldson for your unwavering support and professional advice; Aisha Richards for your continued encouragement; my dear friend Aruna Mathur for years of support, kindness and good wine; David Tennant-Eyles – your creativity, flair and vision was more inspirational than I ever told you; Yael (Elli Dean) for being a great listener and advisor throughout my career; Richard (Mr H) Holder for your decades of friendship and motivation – we are truly ol' skool; and Lisa McQuilkin for being a voice I can depend on and showing me how to question and push boundaries.

And finally, a big thanks to *you* for choosing this book.